THE SOLUTION

THE SOLUTION

GR8 RELATIONSHIPS

EQUIP PRESS

Colorado Springs

THE SOLUTION

Published by Equip Press, Colorado Springs, CO

First Edition: 2023
The Solution / (GR8 Relationships)
Paperback ISBN: 978-1-958585-67-2
eBook ISBN: 978-1-958585-68-9

EQUIP PRESS
Colorado Springs

CONTENTS

INTRODUCTION

You have always been told there's a Solution for every problem, right? But do you sometimes wonder if there is a problem with broken relationships that can be fixed? Can you really have a great relationship with one person? Is it so simple?

At GR8 Relationships, we think you can. But it starts with a bit of work.

Let's dive in.

The Solution for creating GR8 Relationships starts with accurate definitions. Think about your definition of a great relationship. Write it down. Using your definition, list three relationships by name that you consider adequate and inadequate. For this exercise, *adequate* means the relationship meets your definition of a great relationship. *Inadequate* means it does not meet your definition of a great relationship.

Thinking about those relationships and the other person involved, would that person agree with your assessment of the relationship as adequate or inadequate? Would they agree with you concerning whether the relationship is working or not? If they have a different perception than you, what could that mean?

Clearly, being in a relationship with someone who views it differently than you can create great pain and difficulty in the relationship. When both parties have a similar, trustworthy, and valid definition of a great relationship, a truly great relationship is more likely. Robert Fritz calls this the *math* of relationships, meaning it takes two to say *yes* and one to say *no*. When both parties say yes, that is great for the relationship; when either person says no, the two people have little chance for a solid relationship.

Even if you are doing everything right for a great relationship, if the other person isn't, you can influence their ineffective behavior by remaining focused on what God wants you to do in the relationship. Let's consider the biblical direction to a husband and wife regarding what the scripture says about their relationship.

> *Wives, submit to your own husbands, as to the Lord. For the husband is head of the wife, as also Christ is head of the church; and He is the Savior of the body. Therefore, just as the church is subject to Christ, so let the wives be to their own husbands in everything.*
>
> *Husbands, love your wives, just as Christ also loved the church and gave Himself for her . . .*

Ephesians 5:22-25, NKJV

To the wife, God states that she is to respect or submit to the husband. To the husband, God states that he is to love his wife as Christ loves the church. Therefore, it is common to hear something like this from the husband, "I would love her if she would respect me." Or from the wife, "I would respect him if he showed he loved me."

Understanding this foundational underpinning is the first step for GR8 Relationships. The challenge we all run into is the fact that we are human. The way He calls us to interact with each other may not be what we observed growing up or what we were taught by the world, or even the church.

Common Problems

However, before we talk about solutions, let's take a step back and look at some of the common problems caused by trying to change the other person in the relationship. This is triggered by the Flashing ME, which you have learned about in other books in this series.

Finger Pointing

When working with a couple I often ask them to look at each other, extend their arm toward the other person, and point their index finger at each other. Now that they are pointing their finger at each other, I ask one person to say to the other, "If you would just change, I'd be happy."

Then I ask the other person to say, "If you would just change, I would be happy."

Then I ask them to repeat the exercise with both of them saying that phrase at the same time. Generally, everyone laughs after they do the exercise. Most people agree that they do, or have in the past, pointed at the other person in a relationship as the problem. If only *they* would change, everything would be fine.

The simplicity of this exercise emphasizes that the *Problem* of making everything about *ME*, or the *Flashing ME* is real.

Dr. Marlin Howe used to say, "To the degree to which we deny our own issues, we will find a scapegoat on which to dump them."

In my life, that has been absolutely true! It is so easy to direct my thoughts to what's wrong with the other person when I need to make substantial changes. Everyone else is messed up, but not ME! Everyone else needs to change, but not ME! Sounds a bit like a victim, doesn't it?

Here's a critical question about finger-pointing. Think about your closest relationships. Do you think that if the other person would just change, you would be happy, or at least happier?

Why is this thinking not helpful? Because you are ignoring personal responsibility in the relationship. When you allow yourself to ignore the change you need to make in your life you are essentially saying, "The other person is the problem, not me."

If you spend your energy thinking about the changes someone else needs to make, but little or no energy reflecting on what you need to change, you think the other person needs to change more than you do. It is so much easier to see problems in others and even blame them for the problems in your life than to look at yourself.

Consider asking yourself this critical question: "Am I seeking to change others, or me?" Your answer will show whether your relationships are about freedom or control. Freedom can lead to accepting, valuing, and loving others as they are.

Judgmental Behavior

Justice without mercy could be a definition of judgmental behavior. People who are judgmental display hypocritical and self-righteous condemnation of other people rather than an accurate appraisal of the person's character based on their conduct.

Only God can provide both justice and mercy in the right proportion for each situation. People with judgmental behavior tend to *throw the book* at someone, justified in their declaration of someone else's guilt without considering any mercy.

The definition of judgmental behavior as justice without mercy should help change your attitude and actions. Still, the following verse can help you repent, because being judgmental has a big downside.

With what judgment you judge, you will be judged; and with the measure you use, it will be measured back to you.

Matthew 7:2, NKJV

Part of God's plan is that whatever judgment you give will be the very way you are judged. If you have been exacting, unforgiving, and harsh in your relationship with others, you will be measured—or judged—by God in that same manner. The way you judge others is how God will judge you. This eternal law works from God's throne down to us.

With the merciful You will show Yourself merciful;

With a blameless man You will show Yourself blameless; With the pure You will show Yourself pure;

And with the devious You will show Yourself shrewd. For You will save the humble people,

But will bring down haughty looks.

Psalm 18:25-27, NKJV

This below verse is even more specific.

Therefore you are inexcusable, O man, whoever you are who judge, for in whatever you judge

*another you condemn yourself; for you who judge
practice the same things.*

Romans 2:1, NKJV

God looks not only at the act itself, but also at the
possibility of committing it, which He sees by looking
at our hearts. The reason we see hypocrisy, deceit, and a
lack of genuineness in others is that all of them exist in
our own hearts.

A critical characteristic of a believer is humility, as
evidenced by being able to honestly say, "Yes, I would
have exhibited all those behaviors, as well as other evils,
if it were not for the grace of God. Therefore, I have no
right to judge."

If God judged us in the same way we judge others,
we would be condemned to hell. Yet God judges us on
the basis of the miraculous atonement by the Cross of
Christ.

Rather than finding scapegoats, start looking at
your heart. You should let God deal with others and
open your heart to God working on you. That is the
best place to be!

Give it to God Exercise

This exercise will help you move away from
judgmental behavior.

Select any personal relationship you have and write
down the changes you want to see in that other person.

When you are finished writing, find a quiet and private place away from other people.

Fold the sheet of paper and place it in your open hands with your palms facing upward so you are not holding on to it. Then pray something like the following prayer:

> *Lord, You alone are the one responsible for changing people. If You so desire to change (person's name), that is Your business, Your decision, Your will. I want Your will, not mine. I now give this list to You. I desire by Your grace, that You remove my focus and energy from trying to change (person's name) and focus that energy on doing what You want me to do for (person's name) and on serving them. LORD, CHANGE ME. Lord, make me a faithful servant and disciple of yours. I no longer want to waste energy trying to change (person's name). I want to love, accept, and value them where they are, even if they never change. Amen.*

When you finish, spend some time writing down your thoughts and feelings. Most likely you will experience relief, because you are releasing to God your attempt to control someone, and focusing instead on your behavior before God. He is much more interested in the other person than you will ever be.

How much relief you get depends on your view of God. If you see Him as wanting to help, but limited in His ability or desire to help, you will have some, but not much, relief. On the other hand, if you know Him as perfect, powerful, and personal, then your relief will be significant. Your relief will be noticeable as long as you give the changes back to God.

> *Now to Him who is able to do exceedingly*
> *abundantly above all that we ask or*
> *think, according to the power that works in us,*

Ephesians 3:20. NKJV

Trusting God to work His best in others gives you more energy to focus on how He can impact you and what He needs to change in you. This establishes energy for the real relationship. Accept the other person for who they are. It's not your job to change them. Leave that up to God. God loves, values and accepts you for who you are right now, not who you will be.

Consider memorizing the following statement adapted from R.C. Sproul, American Reformed theologian and Radio broadcast host:

> *The heart of a relationship is to know others for*
> *who they are and still value, accept, and love*
> *them.*

Accepting others just as they are (the way God does) is a great precursor for the topic of love. After all, love is The Solution for relationships.

A WORKING
DEFINITION OF LOVE

Now that we have looked at the definition of relationships, let's look at the definition for love.

At GR8 Relationships, we define love as "Pursuing their best patiently, kindly, sacrificially, and unconditionally." This is the cornerstone of the foundation of what we teach.

The opposite of this is acting according to the Flashing ME, which is always self-focused and self-absorbed: The Problem.

Before you read the below scriptures, think about a relationship with someone close to you, where the relationship needs help. As you read the verses, reflect on that relationship.

> *Love suffers long and is kind; love does not envy;*
> *love does not parade itself, is not puffed up;*
> *does not behave rudely, does not seek its own,*
> *is not provoked, thinks no evil; does not rejoice*
> *in iniquity, but rejoices in the truth; bears*

all things, believes all things, hopes all things,
endures all things.

I Corinthians 13: 4-7, NKJV

People who have been around church for any time
at all have likely heard or read the above scripture. Yet
do they apply it? Even if people know and can quote
scripture, it doesn't mean they are applying it to their
lives. The below quotes are poignant when talking about
God's view of love.

> *We have just enough religion to make us hate,*
> *but not enough to make us love one another.*

Jonathan Swift, Irish Clergyman

> *A clear head and a deep understanding are of no*
> *value without a benevolent and charitable heart.*

Matthew Henry, Bible Commentator

We all must start loving God's way rather than the
world's way. Let's explore the world's view of love.

The World's View of Love

The world completely misses the beauty of love
according to God's definition of it. Here are a few bad
descriptions of love.

Love is friendship plus sex.

Havelock Ellis, Physician

Love, as it exists in society, is nothing more than the exchange of two fantasies and the contact of two skins.

Nicola Chamfort, French Writer

Many a man has fallen in love with a girl in a light so dim he would not have chosen a suit by it.

Maurice Chevalier, French Singer

Generally, the world's view of *love* is selfish, conditional, and temporary. This view promotes the Flashing ME, where someone seeks their own good above others.

First, rather than being kind, which would indicate thinking of others, worldly love wants to control others. This love has that Flashing ME on the forehead, which means the person is just after what suits them and makes them feel good.

Second, the world's view of love is dependent on your needs being met. As long as that is happening, you are okay. What's worse is the conditions constantly change because your expectations keep changing. When you were first attracted to someone the conditions were few. Once you know the other person better, your expectations are more intense and numerous. The person saying "I love you," is no longer enough. You need scientific proof!

Finally, both selfish and conditional love lead to temporary love. When you are unhappy, when things get uncomfortable or difficult in the relationship, or when you no longer feel loved or loving, love is gone. It is fleeting as magic fairy dust that is blown away in high wind. It knows nothing of patience.

This temporary condition drives the common misconception of *falling in love*. When you fall, it is not something you decided to do, it happened to you, right? When you fall in love, it just happens to you, you are caught in a wave of feelings, you are sprinkled with love dust and poof, you are now in love! I am not denying the idea of *chemistry* between people. It is real, but that is attraction, not love. And if you can *fall in love*, obviously, you can *fall out of love*. When the love dust is gone, you no longer love them. So, love is seen as a force of the universe that stays with you, or it does not.

When you look at the world's selfish, conditional, and temporary love, it is easy to reject, and desire love to be different. But how often do you relate to others that way?

What is your definition of love? How do you go about loving people in your life?

God's View of Love

Webster's dictionary lists the following definitions of the word *love*:

- A strong affection for one another.
- Attraction based on sexual desire.
- Affection based on admiration.
- Warm attachment or devotion.
- Unselfish loyal & benevolent concern for the good of another.
- An amorous episode between two people.
- A sexual embrace.

Only one of these comes close to the definition of love found in 1 Corinthians 13 (quoted in the previous section), or Ephesians 5.

> *Therefore be imitators of God as dear children. And walk in love, as Christ also has loved us and given Himself for us, an offering and a sacrifice to God for a sweet-smelling aroma.*

Ephesians 5:1-2, NKJV

At GR8 Relationships we use the following definition of love, based on scripture:

> *Pursuing their best (highest good) patiently, kindly, sacrificially and unconditionally.*

Imagine how your life might change if you intentionally applied this definition to all the relationships in your life? Living according to the above definition of love will definitely solve the problem of the Flashing ME because the focus shifts to others who you are in a relationship with. You would no longer be trapped by operating on opinions and emotions, keeping the past in the present, wearing a mask, and trying to change others.

Most importantly, notice this definition gives no conditions to the one who is loved. It does not pursue their best *as long as they pursue my best, too.* A person living by this definition does not limit the suffering, kindness, sacrifice he or she is willing to give, proportionally to how well the other person behaves. Christ is the supreme example of this definition of love, and He practiced it perfectly.

He loved us patiently, kindly, sacrificially, and unconditionally while we were still sinners (Romans 5:6), while we were spiritually dead (Ephesians 2:4, 5), while we were even his enemies (Romans 5:10)! There is no way we will ever be able to pay Him back or be worthy of His love. And still, He loves us!

This is the love He calls you to have for others. This is the love that satisfies because it is not dependent on others. This is the love that transforms horrible relationships into relationships of beauty, hope, and freedom.

The very next time you say, "I love you" ask yourself, "Am I willing to pursue their best, their highest good patiently, kindly, sacrificially, and unconditionally?"

The critical difference between real love and the world's love is the word *decision*. Love is a decision to which your feelings respond. Love exists beyond attraction. It requires a decision to pursue their best, their highest good patiently, kindly, sacrificially, and unconditionally.

Love Solves the Problem

Here are some attributes of great relationships that result from God's true definition of love being applied. These relationships:

- *Don't* require changes or have agendas for others.
- *Don't* require that others have a *job* to fulfill you or make you happy.
- *Do* practice freedom and choice: both parties are free to make bad choices.
- *Do* serve the other person, pursuing their best, which means telling them the truth, even when they may not want to hear it

And, most of all,

- Practice a Godly workable definition of love that makes you personally responsible for your actions toward others and independent of others' actions toward you.

A great relationship is possible only when both parties use something like this working definition of love. There is no dependence on the other person, it only depends on a decision to pursue the other person's best.

When the other person does not practice the definition to pursue your best, that is when your decision is tested. When the other person pursues your best and you cannot see it or do not like it, that is when your decision is tested.

That is why subjects like transformation, freedom, forgiveness, confession, feelings, designs, and judgments are included in this book. Understanding these other items helps you maintain that decision. But nothing is more important for relationships than your decision to apply the definition described here.

You will not be able to practice that definition with your own strength for the long term. Your sin nature will fight against you practicing the definition of love. *Only the Holy Spirit* can provide you the energy to maintain love for the long term.

REFLECTIVE QUESTIONS

- Think about your description of a great relationship before you read this chapter. How much would it change if you used the working definition of love described in this chapter? How would it change if you required nothing of the other person?

_____

_____

_____

_____

- Think about how you define love. How is that impacting your closest relationships?

_____

_____

_____

- What have you learned about God's definition of love that can impact those closest relationships in a positive way?

_____

_____

_____

- If you are a businessperson, how can you apply God's definition of love to business relationships?

_____

_____

_____

_____

THE SOLUTION'S INGREDIENTS

The classic biblical passage describing love is 1 Corinthians 13:4-7. (As with all verses in the Bible, looking at the context helps you understand the verses you read. So, stop now and review chapters 1 through 12 in your Bible before looking at chapter 13.)

Now, let's look at the first three verses in chapter 13:

> *Though I speak with the tongues of men and of angels, but have not love, I have become sounding brass or a clanging cymbal. And though I have the gift of prophecy, and understand all mysteries and all knowledge, and though I have all faith, so that I could remove mountains, but have not love, I am nothing. And though I bestow all my goods to feed the poor, and though I give my body to be burned, but have not love, it profits me nothing.*

I Corinthians 13:1-3, NKJV

The Corinthian church had numerous problems, and these first three verses represent some of the problems. Paul talks about speaking in tongues, knowing all mysteries, having all knowledge, having all faith, bestowing goods to the poor, and even burning their body. That last one sounds awful, but notice what Paul says about all of them.

- Speaking with tongues of men and angels, but no love means I have become just a clanging cymbal.
- Possessing the gift of prophecy, understand all mysteries, all knowledge, all faith, but have no love, I am nothing.
- Bestowing all goods or burning my body, but I have no love, it profits me nothing.

What is happening with them? The Corinthians were making everything about ME, their ME was flashing. They wanted (1) to speak well and sound good (not be a clanging cymbal), (2) to be *somebody* because of their gifts (not be insignificant or nothing), and 3) to profit or be rewarded because of their actions (not be without gain).

But instead of benefitting from their gifts, they were creating problems with their gifts because they were selfish, and not loving.

These first three verses set up the contrast of a self-absorbed life to the supernatural, Holy Spirit energized, others-focused life. God provides the contrast between a life of nothing to a life that has meaning, purpose and rewards.

The meaningful life comes from *pursuing their best patiently, kindly, sacrificially, and unconditionally.* This is a life driven by love and *the most excellent way.* Not based on what you have but based on pursuing the best for others.

Two Primary Components to Be Something

Love is so unlike what the world calls love. You could spend your entire life unpacking the biblical definition of love provided in 1 Corinthians 13:4-7. While you may be familiar with the verses they are far more important than something to read at weddings or hang as a framed needlepoint on the wall! In this passage are fifteen components of the SOLUTION, how to create and maintain a great relationship, and the antidote to self-serving attitudes.

> *Love suffers long and is kind; love does not envy;*
> *love does not parade itself, is not puffed up;*
> *does not behave rudely, does not seek its own,*
> *is not provoked, thinks no evil; does not rejoice*
> *in iniquity, but rejoices in the truth; bears*
> *all things, believes all things, hopes all things,*
> *endures all things. Love never fails.*

I Corinthians 13: 4-8, NKJV

Some theologians think that the first two elements, *suffering long* and *kindness*, are the primary components of the passage and the following thirteen can be classified under one or the other. Let's look at each of these attributes of the solution more closely.

One—Love Suffers Long

How many people would willingly sign up for suffering long?

> *Therefore, as the elect of God, holy and beloved, put on tender mercies, kindness, humility, meekness, longsuffering; bearing with one another, and forgiving one another, if anyone has a complaint against another; even as Christ forgave you, so you also must do.*

Colossians 3:12-13, NKJV

Patience is a great word, but the older term *longsuffering* or *suffering long* provides a clearer picture. "Patience" might bring to mind waiting calmly in a line or not responding when someone has been rude to you. Those are good things to do. But the pain suffered in those situations is usually temporary. Suffering long, on the other hand, speaks of months and years, not minutes and hours.

Suffering long is like the marathon runner who trains with dedication and endurance. Or, how about the picture of a 70-year-old man who still prays for the salvation of his 45-year-old son? Maybe you have suffered long with years of difficulties with your husband or wife. Or can you see your spouse, friends, and relatives that have suffered long with you?

Love has an enormous capacity to be wronged time after time and not retaliate. When you love, you endure evil and injury without resentment, indignation, or revenge. You put up with slights and neglects from the person you love. You wait and hope for the change in the other person, rather than lashing out in resentment at their behavior. You hope for their best and are not fearful of the worst. You wait, for years if needed, without demands, without agendas, without expectations. As Winston Churchill says, "By swallowing evil words unsaid, no one has ever harmed his stomach."

Suffering long is *not* a martyr-like face with a bad attitude, grudgingly gritting your teeth. It is not even patiently taking pain you rightfully deserve. Peter makes this clear:

> *For what credit is it if, when you are beaten for your faults, you take it patiently? But when you do good and suffer, if you take it patiently, this is commendable before God. For to this you were called, because Christ also suffered for us, leaving us an example, that you should follow His steps:*

"Who committed no sin, nor was deceit found in His mouth";

who, when He was reviled, did not revile in return; when He suffered, He did not threaten, but committed Himself to Him who judges righteously; who Himself bore our sins in His own body on the tree, that we, having died to sins, might live for righteousness—by whose stripes you were healed.

1 Peter 2:20-24, NKJV

When you choose to suffer long you reflect Christ by following His example! This involves pursuing the best for others, going the distance with them, and suffering long for them as Christ did for you.

The life of Christ and the energy of the Holy Spirit gives you the power to suffer long, to not give in to angry passions that focus on protecting yourself or getting your way rather than serving others. When you suffer long, you accept that God rewards you for waiting patiently for His timing.

Peter tells us about the reward of longsuffering. It is the capstone and summary of Peter's instructions to suffer long, whether the relationship is with unbelievers, governing authorities, masters/employers, or spouses.

Finally, all of you be of one mind, having compassion for one another; love as brothers,

*be tenderhearted, be courteous; not returning
evil for evil or reviling for reviling, but on the
contrary blessing, knowing that you were called to
this, that you may inherit a blessing. For he who
would love life and see good days, let him refrain
his tongue from evil, and his lips from speaking
deceit.*

1 Peter 3:8-10, NKJV

The blessing you receive is loving life and having good days! That means the sacrifice of suffering long becomes, in one sense, no sacrifice at all!

Two—Love Is Kind

Kindness is valued by most people, but the application of it is often lacking. How much you practice it indicates whether it is just a word, or a value you have. You may say you value fitness, but never workout. That means it is a synthetic value; it's not real, it's just words.

Kindness is enormous in God's economy and a critical component of love. Consider the following.

*And be kind to one another, tenderhearted,
forgiving one another, even as God in Christ
forgave you.*

Ephesians 4:32, NKJV

Kindness demonstrates graciousness toward others. You show them favor. You see and seek opportunities to be helpful and do good for them. You give liberally, not expecting or requiring anything in return. You respect and show consideration for others.

New Testament usage focuses on four facets of kindness: friendliness, compassion, helpfulness, and forbearance.

Dr. Ralph F. Wilson, Director, Joyful Heart™ Renewal Ministries

No wonder kindness is used as one of the elements to describe love.

Where suffering long is marked by the absence of anger under provocation, kindness is a special grace to go further and actively pursue the other person's good, even their best.

But the wisdom that is from above is first pure, then peaceable, gentle, willing to yield, full of mercy and good fruits, without partiality and without hypocrisy.

James 3:17, NKJV

The Old Testament often uses a word for kindness translated as *mercy* or *lovingkindness*. Those two words most often describe God's actions toward the nation of

Israel, ever generous and forbearing. In the same way, He invites you to have a heart of kindness that desires and works for the benefit of others.

> *Life is mostly froth and bubble, two things stand like stone, kindness in another's trouble, courage in your own.*

Adam Lindsay Gordon, Australian Poet

Relationship of the Two Components

These two components are like mercy and grace. Suffering long is like mercy. Kindness is like grace. Suffering long withholds punishment. Kindness gives unmerited favor. Suffering long walks the mile without complaint or measuring stick. Kindness cheerfully volunteers to walk the second mile.

God shows longsuffering and mercy in not treating you as your sins deserve. He shows kindness and grace in giving you abundant life and blessings you could never earn.

If you decided to adopt suffering long and kindness as values, you would offer your relationships the potential to blossom! Be honest, and do not rationalize your behavior with your answers to these questions: Am I putting up with slights and neglects? Am I inclined to show favor, no matter what? If you practice these two qualities, all the other attributes of love will likely become real in your life.

The thirteen words that follow *patient* and *kind* are details about each of the first two words. Here is the way that I see the order.

Eight Ways Love is Patient	Five Ways Love is Kind
• Love does not envy	• Love rejoices in the truth
• Love does not parade itself	• Love bears all things
• Love is not puffed up	• Love believes all things
• Love does not behave rudely	• Love hopes all things
• Love does not seek its own	• Love endures all things
• Love is not provoked	
• Love thinks no evil	
• Love does not rejoice in evil	

Three—Love Does Not Envy

The book of James has a verse that you will see more than once is this book series. It is one of the strongest verses in the Bible that describes what a self-absorbed life leads to:

> *For where envy and self-seeking exist, confusion and every evil thing are there.*

James 3:16, NKJV

The combination of envy and self-seeking is deadly to relationships. Self-seeking, self-absorbed living is a common sickness for all mankind; when envy is added, it becomes a nightmare.

Another word often combined with envy is jealousy. Both are part of a self-absorbed life, but the focus of each word is quite different. Envy is focused on what others have, while jealousy focuses on keeping others away from what you see as yours. It would be like saying, "I want what you have, but you stay away from what I have."

Love does not compare what you have with what they have. Why? Love is *not* about serving *ME*; it is about pursuing the best for others. Love does not resent others for their gifts, honors, or material blessings but rather rejoices for them. It does not feel inferior because such feelings only come from comparison. If you are feeling inferior, that is only because you are comparing what you have to what others have, so envy may be lurking or already present.

In 1 Corinthians 12, Paul addresses envy, self-seeking, and jealousy related to spiritual gifts. When you read 1 Corinthians 12:4-7, the answer is to focus on serving, not comparing. The answer is understanding how you fit into a body of believers to contribute rather than get something from others.

> *There are diversities of gifts, but the same Spirit. There are differences of ministries, but the same Lord. And there are diversities of activities, but it is the same God who works all in all. But the manifestation of the Spirit is given to each one for the profit of all:*

1 Corinthians 12:4-7, NKJV

The focus of love is external, serving and pursuing the best for others. That requires a clear mind to remember that God has given you everything for life and godliness, as we see in 2 Peter. So, envy is not only flawed thinking but also wasted energy.

> As His divine power has given to us all things
> that pertain to life and godliness, through the
> knowledge of Him who called us by glory and
> virtue,

2 Peter 1:3, NKJV

Four—Love Does Not Parade Itself

> A proud man is always looking down on things
> and people; and, of course, as long as you are
> looking down, you cannot see something that is
> above you.

C.S. Lewis

You probably have experienced a time when someone was talking about their proficiency, when you know you are more accomplished at the particular activity. The natural tendency is to find an opening to describe your abilities, right? It is only fitting to let them know how they compare to you, right? Hopefully, that is not one of your common behaviors, but it will be when you follow your sin nature. Self-love, parading yourself, flashing your *ME* makes sure everyone else knows about *ME*!

It is amazingly easy to notice when others are parading themselves, flashing their *ME*. Keep in mind the picture of a *ME* flashing on your forehead. You do not see it as easily as others. The only way to know it is flashing is to look into the mirror of reality or truth by asking yourself, "Am I especially fond of discussing my stuff or my abilities? Do I make sure my talents and good deeds are noticed and properly praised? Oh, how silly, I don't do that . . . or do I?"

Be careful not to rationalize bad behavior. You either want truth or you do not!

This happens in subtle ways, also. Even a right deed done with the wrong motive can be your own little parade. That is the difference between entertaining and hospitality. Entertaining is a show, while hospitality seeks to serve others, be it with china dishes or paper plates.

Another verse that is a favorite of ours describes a Christlike mind.

> *Let nothing be done through selfish ambition or conceit, but in lowliness of mind let each esteem others better than himself.*

> **Philippians 2:3, NKJV**

When you love, you are not interested in esteeming yourself, you are not boastful, conceited, or a braggart, because you want what is best for others and, more importantly, want to glorify God. You do not consider yourself above others, honoring yourself, or parading yourself, because you do not have an "I" problem.

Five—Love Is Not Puffed Up

What do you see when I ask you to picture a peacock, a puffer fish, or a person sticking out their chest? What about a hot air balloon?

There is beauty when you look at those pictures, except for the one where the person is sticking out their chest. Why doesn't that demonstrate beauty like the others? Because there is a difference between calling attention to yourself and just demonstrating the beauty of God's creation.

A peacock is calling attention to itself not because of pride about how it looks, the peacock is fulfilling God's design. The same is true of the puffer fish and, to a degree, the hot air balloon.

The person sticking out their chest or calling attention to themselves is not beautiful. So many athletes act boastful nowadays, and it is ugly. Of course, there is fun in some of that, but despite the fun, it still presents a message of *all about ME*.

Love is not that way. It does not call attention to itself. It does not need to because it is beautiful. It is full of God's wisdom and focuses your attention on Him. Love can remind you how small you are and how great He is, and that all that you have He has gifted by grace.

> *Now these things, brethren, I have figuratively transferred to myself and Apollos for your sakes, that you may learn in us not to think beyond what is written, that none of you may be puffed up on behalf of one against the other. For who makes you differ from another? And what do you have that you did not receive? Now if you did indeed receive it, why do you boast as if you had not received it?*

I Corinthians 4:6-7, NKJV

Love is full of joy for others and concern for their highest good. Even if you are talented, accomplished, or powerful, when you are filled with pride or obsessed with yourself, it detracts from your accomplishments. Since it is common for everyone to focus on ME, when others hear what you say about yourself, especially if you are boastful, they will likely tune out or discount what you say.

> *Be kindly affectionate to one another with brotherly love, in honor giving preference to one another.*

Romans 12:10, NKJV

Six—Love Does Not Behave Rudely

Rude means demeaning, thoughtless, or beyond the boundary of decency. That most likely describes one or more of your actions in the last few days. And those are the things that Satan loves to remind you of, drag you down, and accuse you of being no different than the people of the world.

Satan would have less to bring to mind if you acted rudely and thoughtlessly less of the time. You can only reduce those actions with the power of the Holy Spirit in your life. Yes, you may be able to reduce them temporarily, but not long term, because your sin nature drives your rude and thoughtless actions. The Spirit wars against that behavior as you follow Him. He provides the energy to love and pursue others' best, instead of being rude.

But your mouth provides an easy path to being rude:

> *Let no corrupt word proceed out of your mouth,*
> *but what is good for necessary edification, that it*
> *may impart grace to the hearers.*

Ephesians 4:29, NKJV

The power of the tongue is described in James 3:2-12, and I am pretty sure you know the power from your own experience. I know that I do. Be incredibly careful of sarcasm, which is most often rudeness, beyond the boundary of decency, but just covered over with humor.

Love is courteous, respectful, considerate, and gallant. Love honors authorities, the elderly, and those weaker than you. Love gives men the power to be gentle and protective of women and the power for women to be respectful, gracious, and pure to men.

Love does not value one person over another and respects every person's position, whether you like the person's behavior or not. Imagine the benefit you can provide to others in this rude and indecent world by deciding to pursue their best.

Seven—Love Does Not Seek Its Own

Seeking its own is the *lover of self* problem—and it's a problem for everyone. The billions of dollars spent in the educational system and corporate training programs to promote self-esteem work more against society than for it. If you accept God's Word it is apparent all people are born with a sin nature focused on their flashing ME rather than helping others. Research shows a clear correlation between hostility and high self-esteem, thus the reason you find criminals with high self-esteem. When you pursue your best, it often contradicts what others see as their best, therefore, increasing the probability of hostility.

Love and selfishness are opposites, even enemies because they represent God and Satan. God is love, and Satan is about pride, self-absorption, and flashing ME. Satan continually seeks his way rather than depend on God.

On the other hand, love never seeks to hurt or neglect others. It strives for others' welfare, satisfaction, and advantage. It pursues their highest good. And the outstanding benefit is satisfaction and fulfillment.

Think about that. When you seek your own, you want satisfaction and fulfillment, but it is, at best, temporary, and more likely it does not happen. It is temporary because self is plugged into this world system ruled by Satan, which is all temporary.

But when you pursue the best for others, you operate from an eternal perspective. That is where long-term (even eternal) satisfaction and fulfillment come in. When you pursue the highest good for others your reward is satisfaction that lasts and is renewed by God eternally.

Consider this scenario: You are selfish and self-absorbed, looking to be satisfied. You indulge in your appetites, impulses, and pleasures and are satisfied. Since the fulfillment was based on something temporary, the satisfaction will be temporary. Indulging in materialism, sex, drugs, and alcohol can only provide temporary satisfaction due to their physical and temporal properties.

Worse yet, the dependence on the temporary item can quickly escalate because you want the satisfaction again. But the object of the satisfaction is temporary and invariably the satisfaction is increasingly fleeting the more you rely on it. You can continue to rely on it and allow your appetites, impulses, and pleasures to drive you into something that promises more satisfaction. But the satisfaction acts like a Ponzi scheme that eventually collapses.

Instead of seeking your own benefit, suppose you pursue their best and it helps them. It may be satisfying to you and them. Or you do the same thing, and they do not recognize the benefit. This can still be satisfying to you because you do not depend on them acknowledging you to feel satisfied.

On the other hand, when you do what God wants, you will always be satisfied. He is the living water, contrasted against the earthly water, which satisfies for a while and then satisfies less the more you drink. When you learn to put all of your emotions and pleasure into doing what God asks, you find true satisfaction that no longer depends on life, circumstances, or people.

As you desire to please Him God may reward you further when people benefit from you serving them. Some people will thank you for your service, even though you were not seeking their thanks. God lets you be blessed when you were just doing what He wants you to do. He will also provide you strength, peace, and joy even when others are displeased with you doing the right thing. That is the Christian paradox. By losing your life, you save it. By passing up selfish pleasures, you are everlastingly rewarded.

> *Let them do good, that they be rich in good works, ready to give, willing to share, storing up for themselves a good foundation for the time to come, that they may lay hold on eternal life.*

I Timothy 6:18-19, NKJV

Eight—Love is Not Provoked

The silliest things provoke people. Perhaps it was the gaggle of little girls who insist a boy bothers them, when all he did was grin mischievously at them. Or maybe the same boy gets mad when his favorite cap is snatched, chasing furiously after the cap-snatcher like a cat after a string.

Maybe it is you, when someone said something you disliked, or spoke in *that tone*, and you *had* to tell them how bad their behavior was. Provocation seems to be an art form to some people, and sadly there are too many willing victims because of the prominence of our flashing ME.

You do not have to be a victim controlled by their behavior! You will find freedom in love and choose not to react and respond to people or circumstances. You refuse to allow people to push your *buttons. Buttons* arise from your flashing ME and your need to protect yourself. Love is an outward focus, and there is no ME to protect. Love means trusting God to protect ME, so there is no reason to be defensive about someone else's view of me.

Please note there is a difference between being defensive and defending. Being defensive is taking it personally, flashing your ME. Defending is like 1 Peter 3:15, ". . . be ready to give a defense to everyone who asks you a reason for the hope that is in you, with meekness and fear . . . " Note the manner of the defense: *with meekness and fear.*

When you must be right, flashing your ME, you act defensively, while defending provides persuasive, truth-focused dialogue, which is not led by inappropriate emotions.

There is a place for anger. For example, if a gang is beating a child, that is simply wrong, likely giving rise to anger. But scripture gives a warning to be careful with your anger.

> *"Be angry, and do not sin:" do not let the sun go down on your wrath,*

Ephesians 4:26, NKJV

Most of the time, anger grows from the root of the flashing ME. Next time you are angry slow down and ask, "How am I making this about ME right now?" It will be a rare situation where you are not making it about ME.

It is critical to slow your thinking and emotions down. This will help you change your focus to God's thinking. God wants you to pursue the best for those around you, even if they misunderstand and mistreat you. Love is not provoked because it trusts completely in our *perfect* Father. It does not depend on some superficial tactic like venting, hitting a punching bag, or screaming into a pillow. Those tactics can provide some benefit but rarely offer a solution.

The only solution is to confess your self-seeking ways to God and ask Him to restore a loving (pursuing their best) perspective!

Pursuing their best, loving them, is always the best:

> *It corrects a sharpness of temper, sweetens and softens the mind, so that it does not suddenly conceive, nor long continue, a vehement passion. Where the fire of love is kept in, the flames of wrath will not easily kindle, nor long keep burning. Charity will never be angry without a cause, and will endeavor to confine the passions within proper limits, that they may not exceed the measure that is just, either in degree or duration.*

Anger cannot rest in the bosom where love reigns.
It is hard to be angry with those we love, but very
easy to drop our resentments and be reconciled.

Matthew Henry, Bible Commentator

To be a Christian means to forgive the
inexcusable because God has forgiven the
inexcusable in you.

C.S. Lewis, Christian Author

Nine—Love Thinks No Evil

Godly actions flow from a mind focused intently on the goodness of God. Sooner or later your thoughts will show themselves in your actions, whether evil or good.

Finally, brethren, whatever things are true,
whatever things are noble, whatever things are
just, whatever things are pure, whatever things
are lovely, whatever things are of good report,
if there is any virtue and if there is anything
praiseworthy—meditate on these things.

Philippians 4:8, NKJV

While the sin nature drives evil thoughts, the mind seems to be especially attracted to doing evil when others have wronged you. Those wrongs are not easy to dismiss. They stick in your mind like Velcro and fuel bitterness, resentments, and grudges.

How much more love, joy, and peace might you have if you kept no record of wrongs? If you let go of resentment, grudges, hurts, and thoughts of vengeance? What freedom might come if you dropped your suspicions and plans for revenge, instead focusing on goodness and deeds of kindness? That is the power of forgiveness, driven by the energy of the Holy Spirit and love.

Additionally, love is not inclined to suspect others of evil. This does not mean closing your eyes to evil but simply not suspecting or assuming evil from others. Because of your flashing ME, comparison is built in; therefore, it is easier to believe something terrible about them so you are better, right? That is not love, because love does not compare. Love means pursuing their best, not thinking evil of them. It pursues ways to help and benefit them.

Ten—Love Does Not Rejoice in Evil

This is closely related to the above and could easily be accurate to state that love takes no pleasure in anything wrong. Love is not pleased when evil or pain comes to others, is not happy when others sin, and is not tolerant of any evil. It does not tolerate the lie that calls evil good or harmless and is not afraid of ridicule from standing for the truth. The quote below is relevant for our times.

> *Evil preaches tolerance until it is dominant, then it tries to silence good.*

Archbishop Chaput

Do not confuse tolerating evil with tolerating mistakes. Love makes allowances for the mistakes and sins of others, loving people even in their failings. Love is grieved about evil, even if only from a mistake. Love realizes evil results in pain, grief, and destruction. Love hopes, prays, encourages, and sometimes exhorts and rebukes, and always pursues the highest good of the other person.

> *Let love be without hypocrisy. Abhor what is evil. Cling to what is good.*

Romans 12:9, NKJV

Eleven—Love Rejoices in Truth

Love rejoices when truth prevails. It is not about being right and winning arguments, because that is not love; it is flashing your ME. No, love rejoices in truth for its own sake! Truth brings freedom and light and is always better than lies for those you love. Love is honest and does not fear saying things which, though they may hurt for a time, are nonetheless truths that benefit the other person.

More importantly, when you are exposed to the truth, it is a healing element, even though it may hurt. Love rejoices in truth, because truth is about freedom, which is the reason Christ died for you.

> *And you shall know the truth, and the truth shall make you free.*

John 8:32, NKJV

Twelve—Love Bears All Things

> *. . . love covers a multitude of sins*

I Peter 4:8, NKJV

Not only does God cover sin, He also demonstrates patience. Both of those thoughts are part of *bearing all things*. Thank goodness God loves like this! He hates sin but is patient as He sanctifies you. He is the example of how to relate to others. Love seeks to protect, focuses on the good, forgives wrongs, and works with people to help them overcome their faults. Love bears any difficulty willingly for the good of others and God's glory.

Not publishing the faults of others may be much easier than bearing up under the burden of those you care about, who not only do not show care for you now but are hurting you. Love is not dependent on the object to love back. It is a decision, independent and separate from anything related to them which frees you to care for them when they do not care for you.

This truth is powerful and freeing because you are not trapped into thinking others need to change for your life to get better. You are not dependent on that; instead, you are dependent on the Lord God of the Universe taking care of them and you.

A good picture of bearing all things is in J. R. R. Tolkien's book, *The Return of the King*. Frodo Baggins and Samwise Gamgee have come to the hardest stage of their quest; climbing Mount Doom to destroy the evil Ring. Frodo, who has been carrying the Ring, has no more strength to continue.

> *"Now for it! Now for the last gasp!" said Sam as he struggled to his feet. He bent over Frodo, rousing him gently. Frodo groaned, but with a great effort of will he staggered up; and then he fell upon his knees again. He raised his eyes with difficulty to the dark slopes of Mount Doom towering above him, and then pitifully he began to crawl forward on his hands.*
>
> *Sam looked at him and wept in his heart, but no tears came to his dry and stinging eyes. 'I said I'd carry him if it broke my back," he muttered, "and I will!"*

"Come, Mr. Frodo!" he cried. "I can't carry it for you, but I can carry you and it as well. So up you get! Come on, Mr. Frodo dear! Sam will give you a ride. Just tell him where to go, and he'll go."

As Frodo clung upon his back, arms loosely about his neck, legs clasped firmly under his arms, Sam staggered to his feet; and then to his amazement he felt the burden light. He had feared that he would have barely strength to lift his master alone, and beyond that he had expected to share in the dreadful dragging weight of the accursed Ring. But it was not so. Whether because Frodo was so worn by his long pains, wound of knife, and venomous sting, and sorrow, fear, and homeless wandering, or because some gift of final strength was given to him, Sam lifted Frodo with no more difficulty than if he were carrying a hobbit-child pig-a-back in some romp on the lawns or hayfields of the Shire.

J. R. R. Tolkien

Are you willing to carry someone else's burdens? It will be much lighter than you realize when you depend on God to provide the strength to do it.

Thirteen—Love Believes All Things

The disease of doubt springs from fear. Faith in God is the antidote. If you trust Him, you can know whether people do good or bad God in His sovereignty will use their choices for good. You need not be overwhelmed with pessimism and mistrust, and you don't have to be gullible, either.

> *Indeed charity does by no means destroy prudence, and, out of mere simplicity and silliness, believe every word, Proverbs 14:15. Wisdom may dwell with love, and charity be cautious. But it is apt to believe well of all, to entertain a good opinion of them when there is no appearance to the contrary; nay, to believe well when there may be some dark appearances, if the evidence of ill be not clear.*

Matthew Henry, Bible Commentator

Trust is often linked to the idea of being earned. However, it is most often a gift! Think about the last time you sat in a chair. Did you gingerly test its structural strength and inquire about the credentials and training of the craftsman or manufacturer? No, you just sat, because you trusted the chair! There are so many examples of how much trust is gifted. If it were gifted and then misused, then the trust must be earned.

In the same way, you have the glorious opportunity to believe the best about people first, and even if proven wrong at some point, to believe in God's power, love, and redemption. This is the most crucial idea behind believing all things. You depend on God to deal with people, so it frees you to believe the best.

How about a new way of thinking? Believe badly about others with *utmost* reluctance.

Fourteen—Love Hopes All Things

Love hopes all things is similar to *love believes all things*, but it seems to express a more significant challenge. Suppose there is evidence to doubt. This is where hope enters; hope for turning back to what is good and right. The facts have reduced or removed trust but hope still lingers.

When you pursue their best, you hope and believe God can do amazing works in them, as He does in you. He can turn a heart of cold stone into a vibrant soul passionate about Him, a Saul into a Paul, a slave-trading John Newton into a pastor and writer of *Amazing Grace.*

> *And when, in spite of inclination, it cannot*
> *believe well of others, it will yet hope well,*
> *and continue to hope as long as there is any*
> *ground for it. It will not presently conclude a*
> *case desperate, but wishes the amendment of the*

worst of men, and is very apt to hope for what it wishes.

Matthew Henry, Bible Commentator

[The Christian] does not think God will love us because we are good, but that God will make us good because He loves us.

C.S. Lewis, Christian Author

Are you willing to hope for their best, even if they are currently sinning and caught in a life of doing what is wrong? If so, that is love.

Fifteen—Love Endures All Things

Nothing can deter love. Pain, suffering, loneliness, heartache, loss, and hatred are not strong enough to stop love. Love has no price tag. Nothing can compare to love because it will endure all and outlast all. It perseveres, holds fast, and stands firm in injury and unpleasant circumstances for the sake of others and God.

Note, what a fortitude and firmness fervent love will give the mind! What cannot a lover endure for the beloved and for his sake! How many slights and injuries will he put up with! How many hazards will he run and how many difficulties encounter!

Matthew Henry, Bible Commentator

Looking to Jesus the author and finisher of our faith; who for the joy that was set before him endured the cross, despising the shame, and is set down at the right hand of the throne of God.

Hebrews 12:2, NKJV

The joy set before Christ was your redemption and His glory! In the same way, you can joyfully endure all things.

Love Never Fails—Permanent & Perpetual

What a statement—love never fails! It is permanent and perpetual. No example, evidence, or fact shows love does not work. It not only works, it is also eternal.

And now abide faith, hope, love, these three; but the greatest of these is love.

1 Corinthians 13:13, NKJV

All things will be fulfilled, even faith and hope. Love, however, is everlasting! There is nothing temporary or faddish because it describes God Himself. God is love, and His love for us never fails.

But what about your love? Do you fall in and out of love? Is love temporary? Using our definition of love would mean you *fell into* pursuing their best; patiently, kindly, sacrificially, and unconditionally.

Obviously, love is not that mindless. Falling in and out of love is not love. It may be attraction or something else, but it is certainly not love. Love involves thinking and decisions. When you consider love as a decision, the statement would be "I was attracted to them and now I am no longer." Or maybe more accurately, "I was attracted to them, got to know them, and decided I didn't want to pursue their best." There are numerous permutations, but love is different.

Love never fails. Relationships and marriages will blossom and grow when love is the foundation. Without it, you have the world's view of relationships, as temporary.

When you love, you participate in an ongoing story that will continue throughout eternity. You are, in fact, living the abundant life now!

> *At the end of things, The Blessed will say, "We have never lived anywhere except in Heaven." And the lost will say, "We were always in Hell." And both will speak truly.*

C.S. Lewis, Christian Author

REFLECTIVE QUESTIONS

- Which of the 15 components of love do you need to work on the most? Choose at least two, but no more than five. What in your relationships prompted you to pick the ones you did?

_____

_____

_____

_____

- Reflect on the quote below by C.S. Lewis. How does it apply to your life and relationships?

_____

_____

_____

_____

At the end of things, The Blessed will say, "We have never lived anywhere except in Heaven." And the lost will say, "We were always in Hell." And both will speak truly.

FREEDOM

We all want freedom, don't we? But what gets in the way? In many ways, the Flashing Me gets in the way. Because when you focus on yourself, you end up removing their freedom, your freedom, or both. If you try to get someone to change, most often you are giving them a "job" to do for you. That job is to make you happy by them changing. Is that freedom in a relationship? Or you may want acceptance from some people, so you engage in people-pleasing, but this gets in the way of your freedom because you are now tied to making them happy. Though it may seem like you are focusing on others, you are really focusing on yourself.

So, let's look at freedom. When you are free you can live and support strong relationships. Freedom is a key component of a great relationship, whether between spouses, in a family unit, or among business colleagues.

Freedom Is Not Led by Emotion

Feelings will lie to you. If you would rather live with truth instead of speculation or opinion, then you should be clear about the interaction of three elements:

feelings, thoughts, and actions. The solution, love, is not emotionless, nor is it emotion-led.

Think about your favorite scary movie. The film is structured to draw you into the story, to appeal to your emotions, making you see yourself as one of the characters in the movie. When you remind yourself of reality, your fear is reduced or removed. Your thinking is primarily what your emotions are responding to, therefore, reducing the film's efforts to engage your fear.

So, there are two important implications. *First*, feelings and emotions are primarily *responders*. When you watch a movie and you are scared, sad, happy, or crying, your emotions are responding to the movie. Feelings need something to respond to.

Second, and most important, feelings are **often** untrustworthy. If you can be scared but not be in danger (like watching a movie), then your emotions are untrustworthy. Your emotions are real, but they are responding to something unreal.

Consider the words Think-Feel-Act. Which order do you think people display these? Like it or not, people typically react and respond like an amoeba – a single-cell organism with little or no ability to think. Poke it, and it will move away. Offer sugar, and it will come to you.

> *Jesus said to him, "you shall love the Lord your God with all your heart, with all your soul, and with all your mind." This is the first and great*

*commandment. And the second is like it: "You
shall love your neighbor as yourself. On these
two commandments hang all the Law and the
Prophets."*

Matthew 22:37-40, NJKV

Which happens first in those verses? Everything
depends on what love is. The construction of the
sentence says love is a verb; therefore, action comes first.
Some might say love is a feeling, so God is asking us to
act on a feeling.

Actually, God is asking you to decide. Remember
the working definition of love: "Pursuing their best
patiently, kindly, sacrificially, and unconditionally." That
is a decision! It requires thinking to make a conscious
choice. So, a reasonable conclusion is that *thinking* is
first in those verses.

Before going any further, I want to say I think
emotions and feelings are great! The proper use of
emotion allows us to enjoy the highs and lows of life.
The danger is when you trust your emotions to initiate
actions but do not look for the source of your emotions.

Feelings Can Create Problems

Feelings will often create problems. Feelings are
not bad; they are just indicators. They respond to the
stimuli they receive and are, therefore, untrustworthy
and fickle. Consider the below statements.

- Bad can feel good.
- Good can feel bad.

"Bad can feel good" is easy to prove. You have no doubt experienced feeling good, even excited, as you encounter temptation and sin. But it is followed by an inner conviction that you have done something wrong. This good feeling about doing something bad will always be temporary unless your heart is hardened.

Vengeance is one "bad" that may feel good longer than other sins because your mind is focused on justice and getting even. Most other sins register quickly with regret or guilt, replacing whatever positive emotion existed. The story of any sin fits the "bad can feel good" statement and is clearly illustrated in the original sin in the Garden of Eden.

> So when the woman saw that the tree was good
> for food, that it was pleasant to the eyes, and
> a tree desirable to make one wise, she took of
> its fruit and ate. She also gave to her husband
> with her, and he ate. Then the eyes of both of
> them were opened, and they knew that they were
> naked; and they sewed fig leaves together and
> made themselves coverings.
>
> And they heard the sound of the LORD God
> walking in the garden in the cool of the day,
> and Adam and his wife hid themselves from the

presence of the LORD God among the trees of the
garden.

Genesis 3:6-8, NKJV

Put yourself in Eve's place and let your emotions follow the story. Eve was swept away by the appeal of the fruit that was good for food, pleasant to the eyes, and could make her wise. She felt good about eating the fruit, but it was bad.

And to prove it was bad, notice where their feelings go next. "Their eyes were opened . . . knew they were naked . . . hid themselves . . . " Feelings were responding to the reality of what God said would happen.

"Good can feel bad" is also real. Consider the emotional conflict you experience when you know a close friend or relative is sinning. You know it is time to speak with them, so you gather your courage to do it, but you believe (think) it will end poorly, engaging your emotions to work against you. And, in those cases where the conversation goes badly, you may experience feelings of regret instead of peace or joy for doing what was right.

A good parent disciplining their child understands "good can feel bad." Similarly, when a good leader shares the truth with a person because they are not doing a good job, it often does not feel good.

Since your feelings are only indicators or responders, then either acting or thinking should come first. This choice is rather easy, right? Ready – fire – aim is not a good option. Acting prior to thinking can be as bad as letting your emotions lead.

Thinking / Feeling Principle

Which is easiest to change – thinking or acting? Acting is often chosen and written about, but it is actually thinking. Consider this; thinking about changing our actions precedes the actual actions, right? This does not mean you believe the thinking, but you are acting on it, nevertheless.

The more you act consistently with your thinking, the more it will be reinforced, impacting your beliefs and your feelings. Life can be simplified when you consider the power of thinking. If you think correctly, it will drive good actions and, at some point, good feelings. Unfortunately, if your thinking is bad, it will drive incorrect actions and feelings. So, what you are thinking is especially important!

> *The mind governed by the flesh is death, but the mind governed by the Spirit is life and peace.*

> **Romans 8:6, NIV**

Two great passages about thinking are shown below:

> *I beseech you therefore, brethren, by the mercies of God, that you present your bodies a living*

sacrifice, holy, acceptable to God, which is your reasonable service. And do not be conformed to this world, but be transformed by the renewing of your mind, that you may prove what is that good and acceptable and perfect will of God.

Romans 12:1-2, NKJV

Finally, brethren, whatever things are true, whatever things are noble, whatever things are just, whatever things are pure, whatever things are lovely, whatever things are of good report, if there is any virtue and if there is anything praiseworthy—meditate on these things.

Philippians 4:8, NKJV

Your thinking drives your values and beliefs. Your thinking drives who you trust, what you trust, who you respect, and every choice you make. Even if you disagree with the above statement, please recognize the number of things you can control is minimal.

Regarding the interaction of thinking, feelings, and actions, it is generally best to do the following:
- Think first, then Feel or Act.
- In difficult situations, Think – Act – Feel

Build a solid foundation of good thinking and good values. Then, act based on that foundation. Your feelings will eventually respond.

Thinking that arises from your sin nature, which is wired-in, will always lead to a focus on satisfying yourself rather than glorifying God. Even if you have studied and practiced good thinking from God's Word, any difficult situation or flawed thinking not subjected to Jesus Christ (2 Corinthians 10:4-5) will follow the wiring of the sin nature.

Without the power of the Holy Spirit guiding your thinking, your sin nature will introduce fear, uncertainty, and doubt. How will this impact me? What is going to happen to me and my family? This is the same strategy Satan used on Eve, getting her to question God's promises and goodness.

If you do not have a solid foundation in God's Word, specifically that God is *perfect* and will take care of you, then you will fill your mind with assumptions, speculation, guesses, and opinions that will lead to fear.

Freedom and Choice

Freedom For You

Do you think you are free to be yourself? You may not be as free as you think!

Have you accepted how God made you? Have you accepted the life God has placed you in? Do you spend your energy trying to impress people? Do you avoid sharing the truth with people because you think it will upset them or make them dislike you? Do you walk on eggshells around some people, expecting them to get angry with you or run away in tears at any misspoken word? Are you focused on pleasing people rather than serving them? Are you upset, depressed, or discouraged that life is not as good as it used to be? Do you remind yourself what life could have been if you had not made that wrong decision? Are you worrying and anxious about what is coming tomorrow, next week, next year?

If those types of statements fill your mind, you are not as free as you think!

You are free to make choices and to live good values. God set you free. He has given you the opportunity to know and do what is right, to have joy even in the worst of situations. The proper use of your freedom is ultimately dependent on good and godly thinking. You can be in a physical prison but free in your thinking like the Apostle Paul when he was in jail, because you depend on God. When you believe He allows this circumstance for good, and not for bad, you are not slave to that situation. You are not controlled by it.

Freedom For Others

Do you accept that others are free? When you start learning about freedom, you may hear yourself say, "I am giving them freedom."

Perhaps you do not understand how freedom works. You can only give someone freedom when it is actually in your control. For example, you can give someone a goal to achieve, unlock their cell door, or give them your automobile keys to use your car. But this is not giving them freedom in the way we are discussing it. People are already free to act however they want. That is not something you give; it is something you accept as true.

You may not realize how much you try to control other people. I certainly do not!

Are you mad at them without telling them? Are you discouraged, angry, depressed, or resentful when "They just don't get it"? Are their poor values, bad decisions, or flawed thinking causing you to worry and fret?

That thinking denies the reality of their freedom to act badly, even sin, and experience the consequences. Of course, this may be why you are trying to limit their freedom, so they will not experience the consequences. And, too often, you want to control other people's lives for the wrong reason. If they change, you can relax and be happy, at least for a while.

You claim, "I'm only concerned. Isn't that okay?"

If you answer yes, it may be that you see sin in another person's life and you know sin has consequences. If that is the situation, you hope, pray, encourage, and perhaps exhort and rebuke. You do those things because you know God has asked you to "speak the truth in love" (Ephesians 4:15). You are not doing this to be the Jr. Holy Spirit in their life – you do it because it is pursuing their best.

Or, if your answer is no, it may be you feel compelled to *make* them change. If true, that is where their behavior controls you. You may have the right motive, hoping they change to escape the consequences of the sin, but you see this as your responsibility, not God's and theirs, to change their behavior. Be careful and be objective. Your ME flashing will remove objectivity every time.

Obviously, accepting their freedom does not mean you give up on them changing! Freedom agrees with the reality that changing them is *not your job*. And whether they change or not, your job is to tell the truth, love them, and pursue their best. Change is their job and dependent upon God's plan.

If you decide to control, beware. It *will* hurt your relationships. When you try to control a person, you act as though choice is not available to them. There is no freedom there!

> *You cannot build character and courage by*
> *taking away a man's initiative and independence.*

Abraham Lincoln

<u>REFLECTIVE QUESTIONS</u>

- Consider the options for three words: Think – Feel – Act. Which sequence do you use? How does that impact your relationships?

_____

_____

_____

_____

- Based on the section on your freedom, how free are you really? What do you need to change to become truly free?

_____

_____

_____

_____

- Examine the important relationships in your life. Are you allowing others to be free?

_____

_____

_____

_____

FORGIVENESS

Forgiveness creates freedom from resentments, bitterness, grudges and is a critical component of the Solution in any relationship. We are all human. We all have a sin nature, so we are bound to step on some toes, intentionally or unintentionally. We are likely to have had someone hurt us in our lives. We can tie a rope to the event or situation and run in circles around it or let it go, forgive, and live in freedom.

Benefits of Forgiveness

Forgiveness has many benefits for the forgiver! Forgiveness pleases God.

And be kind to one another, tenderhearted, forgiving one another, just as God in Christ also forgave you.

Ephesians 4:32, NKJV

Does the verse give any options not to forgive? Do you forgive if the other person has met some specific criteria? No! There are no criteria, only an example to follow – God. Forgiving others is like thanking God for forgiving you! We did not deserve it, yet He asked Christ to pay the penalty for our sins, and Christ agreed.

Forgiveness imitates God. It is a divine action. When you forgive, you not only thank God, but also want to act like God, not like your sin nature. It says you trust what He has done, and want to follow His amazing example.

When you forgive, you escape serious consequences. When you forgive, you maintain your walk with God. You cannot love God and hate your brother at the same time.

> *If someone says, 'I love God', and hates his brother, he is a liar; for he who does not love his brother whom he has seen, how can he love God whom he has not seen? And this commandment we have from Him: that he who loves God must love his brother also.*

I John 4:20-21, NKJV

Forgiveness will help you maintain your health and vitality. Psalm 32 was probably written by David after he sinned with Bathsheba and had Uriah killed. While this scripture is more about confession, it still provides the precise impact of the loss of health without forgiveness. Listen to David contrast the joy of forgiveness with the physical suffering of unconfessed sin.

Blessed is he whose transgression is forgiven,
Whose sin is covered.

Blessed is the man to whom the Lord does not
impute iniquity, And in whose spirit there is no
deceit.

When I kept silent, my bones grew old Through
my groaning all the day long.

For day and night Your hand was heavy upon
me;

My vitality was turned into the drought of
summer. Selah I acknowledged my sin to You,

And my iniquity I have not hidden.

I said, "I will confess my transgressions to the
Lord," And You forgave the iniquity of my sin.
Selah

Psalm 32:1-5, NKJV

Forgiveness will help you maintain joy. The only
alternative to forgiveness is vengeance and bitterness.
Think about it; there is no middle ground, no matter
how you try to avoid the issue. So, ask yourself, "Do I
want to forgive or to be bitter and vengeful?"

. . . looking carefully lest anyone fall short of the
grace of God; lest any root of bitterness springing

up cause trouble, and by this many become
defiled . . .

Hebrews 12:15, NJKV

Bitterness and vengeance fuel wars and disputes
you have with your enemies. They are probably at the
heart of your marriage or family struggle. Bitterness and
vengeance always hurt and destroy you as well as others.
Forgiveness, though, heals. Which do you want?

Forgiveness allows you to maintain freedom. If you
do not forgive, you fall into the trap of being consumed
with your offender. How can you be free when you
spend so much time thinking about how they hurt you?
Your mind is stuck on resolving something only God
can handle effectively. The longer you hold the grudge,
the more they control your thoughts, actions, and
feelings. The more you seek vengeance, the more energy
drains from you.

When you become like the offender, you have
completely lost your freedom. The Lord has a better
path for you. He wants you to renew your mind. He
wants your mind controlled by His thinking, by truth.
Most importantly, He does not want you to renew your
mind to just anything; it is to renew your mind to truth.

Forgiveness helps you maintain hope. If you have
an unhealthy focus on past events, you can become
depressed and lose hope. You cannot correct a wrong
that occurred in the past. Forgiveness encourages hope
and a new future for your life.

Forgiveness maintains the health of future generations. Research shows parents' unresolved issues pass on to children. In attitude, words, and actions, your flawed thinking, whether you know it or not, is passed on to your children; even if they learn from your mistakes and do not repeat them, they will still suffer in other ways for your mistakes.

God clearly states this in Exodus.

> . . . *For I, the Lord your God, am a jealous*
> *God, visiting the iniquity of the fathers upon the*
> *children to the third and fourth generations of*
> *those who hate Me.*

Exodus 20:5. NKJV

But, like everything our marvelous Lord does, He provides a solution. There is hope, joy, and blessing if you pay attention to what He says. Exodus 20:6 says,

> . . . *but showing mercy to thousands, to those who*
> *love Me and keep My commandments.*

Exodus 20:6, NKJV

The past is over. Move on! Trust God to redeem your past! He knows what is best for you. And He is using this situation for your best and for the other person's best. Trust His perfection! Doing it any other way will create more problems.

Definition—What it Is, What it Isn't

Forgiveness is showing love instead of seeking revenge when you feel you have been wronged. Here is our working definition of forgiveness: Forgiveness is a choice to lay the offense down, not mark or pay attention to where you laid it and never use it against them, not in your thoughts, speech, or actions. Here is the shorter version to memorize:

Never abusing them for the wrong they did to you, not in thought, word, or action.

It's a process of dealing with hurts so they can heal and you can move forward in freedom. Who is our model for forgiveness? Our savior Jesus who hung on the cross and took our sin on himself. God did not hang onto His wrath for how we, as humans, turned away from Him. He forgave us and provided a way for us to live eternally, starting now as we live our lives.

Forgiveness is not pardoning; it does not deal with justice, that is God's job. Forgiveness never removes the offense; you no longer pay attention to the wrong and do not hold the offense against someone else. Knowing and doing this frees you and potentially the offender from slavery to the pain of the offense.

Forgiveness is not forgetting. If you can forget a wrong, forgiveness is not necessary. Forgiveness heals and leaves scars. Scars indicate the healing process has occurred. Forgiveness means remembering a hurt has healed.

Forgiveness does not mean restoration or reunion. Forgiveness is what happens inside of a person. God may come in to create restoration and reunion, but that is not part of forgiveness. It takes two for restoration or reunion but only one for forgiveness.

Forgiveness is not dependent on the offender's repentance. Some say you do not need to forgive unless the person who wronged you has repented. They can use this passage for support.

> *Take heed to yourselves. If your brother sins against you, rebuke him; and if he repents, forgive him. And if he sins against you seven times in a day, and seven times in a day returns to you, saying, "I repent," you shall forgive him.*

Luke 17:3-4, NKJV

Some people who wrong you will never repent. Think of all the unforgiveness we would drag around every day if we had to wait for someone to repent before we could forgive. God is not removing our freedom by binding us to the actions of another person. And remember, God forgave us at the cross before we were born or repented.

Forgiveness is not interested in my rights. *My rights* originate with the Flashing ME, which proclaims the following.

"My happiness, my rights are far more important than:

- the pain I will create for my spouse,
- the emotional health of and pain on my children,
- the pain that will impact my extended family,
- the scars and pain I will create for my grandchildren,
- even God's Word itself, which says my actions are not right.

My rights or the *Flashing ME* will close our eyes to forgiveness and the solution for all relationships, which is to pursue their best, no matter what, just like Christ does for us.

Process of Forgiveness

The process of forgiveness is like healing a wound. Let's compare the medical steps and the spiritual steps for wound care.

Step One—Face Their Humanity (Stop the Bleeding)

Estimates say 80 percent of what we see lies behind our own eyes. If this is true, then when we're looking at the offender, we mostly see the wrong and the pain, not the person. We see that *animal, jerk, piece of trash*, but we do *not* see the person.

If we want to be free of the pain, we can stop the bleeding by taking this first step. Choose to see people for who they are, not for what they do or did. Rediscover the humanity of the person. Choose to see them differently!

Step Two—Overlook Revenge (Clean the Wound)

Overlook your *assumed* right to revenge or to get even. We think we have the right to revenge, but we do not. Revenge is God's right alone.

> *Repay no one evil for evil. Have regard for good things in the sight of all men. If it is possible, as much as depends on you, live peaceably with all men. Beloved, do not avenge yourselves, but rather give place to wrath; for it is written, "Vengeance is Mine, I will repay," says the Lord.*

Romans 12:17, NKJV

Forgiveness accepts God's justice and does not trust our idea of justice. When we try to be God, we assume the role of avenger! We say we want justice, but from our hand such a thing is impossible. And if we are honest with ourselves, we know we want to do just a bit more to them than they did to us. When we try to get even, we multiply our sin toward the other person and toward God by demanding He get off His throne and allow us to sit in His place. Christ forgave us, and He asks us to forgive others.

. . . bearing with one another, and forgiving
one another, if anyone has a complaint against
another; even as Christ forgave you, so you also
must do.

Colossians 3:13, NKJV

This step is crucial because it is the best chance to go forward. You draw a line in the sand, hand vengeance to God, and move forward. You let God clean the wound.

Step Three—Renew Your Mind (Apply Antibiotic)

Before you entered the first step of forgiveness, your feelings toward the offender may have been hate, bitterness, and anger. You wanted bad things to happen to the bad person who did bad things to you. That is what hate is all about. Since feelings are primarily responders, thinking and actions need to change to revise your feelings. Remember the proper order: think first, then act or feel. Choose to believe truth like the following:

And we know that all things work together for
good to those who love God, to those who are the
called according to His purpose

Romans 8:28, NKJV

God fully understands your situation. He has not been caught off guard. God controls vengeance and the whole situation. Choose to see the offender as an instrument of God. Remember God is using that person to develop and shape you to be more like Jesus Christ. That may be a hard pill to swallow, but if you do not swallow, you are not trusting God. Further, you miss out on blessings that can only come from trusting God through forgiveness.

Joseph is a good example. Remember the mistreatment Joseph suffered because of his brothers? Yet when he was in an ideal position to take full vengeance on them, his response was completely unexpected.

> *Joseph said to them, "Do not be afraid, for am I in the place of God? But as for you, you meant evil against me; but God meant it for good, in order to bring it about as it is this day, to save many people alive. Now therefore, do not be afraid; I will provide for you and your little ones." And he comforted them and spoke kindly to them.*
>
> **Genesis 50:19-21, NKJV**

When we forgive someone, we decide never to use that offense against them or pay attention to it again. We unhand the *weapon* that could be used on them. We give it up, stop grasping, and stop holding onto the offense.

Step 4—Give it Up, Grasp it No More (Cover the Wound)

In this step, you make the following decisions.

- Conclude, commit to stop holding onto the offense against them.
- Conclude, commit to moving forward rather than remain stuck in the past.
- Conclude, commit to blessing them and freeing yourself.
- You decide, conclude, and commit to FORGIVE.

Bitterness keeps us stuck in the past, but forgiveness allows us to move forward into the future. This does not mean we need to forgive and forget, as some people say. Forgetting is not a necessary element of forgiveness, though it sometimes comes afterward.

God does not forget as we do. He is not paying attention to and not marking our sin against us because He sees us through the blood of Jesus. We are accepted because of Jesus' death, burial, and resurrection. Now, our sins are no longer a barrier between God and us. Thank God for that! We can know when God forgives us, He does not use our sin against us ever again.

How about letting it go? God knows what is best for you and this situation. How about "not marking it against them"? Why keep hurting yourself?

A rattlesnake, if cornered, will become so angry it will bite itself. That is exactly what the harboring of hate and resentment against others is – a biting of oneself. We think we are harming others in holding these spites and hates, but the deeper harm is to ourselves.

E. Stanley Jones, American Missionary

It is time to give it up so you can cover the wound and give it a chance to heal.

Step Five—Apply Your Decision (Change the Dressing Regularly)

The scars on your body are memorials of healing!

I have some significant scars on my body from a skiing accident, a near-death experience, as well as two back surgeries. Those situations were extremely painful at the time, but they are not painful now because they are healed!

If I had some lousy thinking, I could look at those scars, remember the pain, and put myself back into the pain and difficulty of each situation. But why would I do that? Those situations are over, and the scars are proof of the healing. Wouldn't it be better to see the scars and remember that the situation is over, and I am healed? This is why we believe in *forgive* and *remember*. Once you have experienced the power of forgiveness, you will have multiple scars – all healed – rather than open wounds.

Forgive and remember help for old as well as new wounds. When you remember or reflect on any old *wound,* you can remember that it is now a scar that is healed, and there is no need to reopen it. When you have a new wound, you can remember the scars and healing from the old wounds. This will help you consider forgiving again, maybe even now.

Unfortunately, without forgiveness we leave the wounds open, and they turn into bloody messes. Not what God wants for you!

Once you have forgiven, whatever you can do to remember the forgiveness, do it! Because in the heat of emotion it is easy to forget. You decide to forgive in Step 4. You have committed to new thinking (no longer revenge) instead, letting it go. Now memorialize that thinking with an action and a date. Think of this step like baptism is for us. Baptism does not save us but is a testimony, a memorial to the most important decision you and I will ever make, to trust God for our eternity.

Here is a good application and remembrance exercise. Write down the name of the person you want to forgive and what is being forgiven on a small card or piece of paper. Take the card and go to a quiet place. Kneel and place the card in your hands, palms up. Hold the card up to heaven. Pray to the Lord in your own words what you have written on the card and tell Him you are forgiving them, and you want Him to take this event from you. Pray anything else you desire about the event, and when you finish, write the date and time on the card. Put the card in a safe place to remind you that you have forgiven the person, or throw the card away if there is a chance the person might see it. But remember the date somehow. Now you have a date, a memorial to remind you that you forgave them.

Step Six—Validate and Verify Your Decision (Look for signs of infection)

Satan and your sin nature are not happy with forgiveness. You will have many opportunities to move backward toward vengeance and bitterness, including the next time you get into an argument, the next time you feel slighted, or the next time you see, hear, smell, taste, or touch something that reminds you of what happened. Anytime you start *Flashing your ME* with the person who wronged you, you may move back toward bitterness. In fact, most likely, immediately after forgiving, the event will cross your mind. Satan, through your sin nature, wants you to *pay attention* to it, to go back to life before you forgave the person.

So, how do you deal with these thoughts about what they did to you? You say you forgave, but the thoughts keep coming up. It depends on the answer to one critical question. Before you ask the critical question, consider these options:

- Option One: You did not forgive when you said you did.

- Option Two: You did forgive and need to forgive again.
- Option Three: You did forgive and need to validate your forgiveness.

All three options beg this critical question, "Did I forgive them when I said I did?"

The answer to the question is either yes or no. "Maybe" is like a no because there will be no freedom. Forgiveness is about freeing you from the bondage of their offense toward you.

Right now, ask that question about the wrong the person did to you. "Did I forgive them when I said I did?" Yes or no?

If your answer is no, ask the Lord to help you understand forgiveness and prepare you to forgive. You can choose to be free or stay in bondage. You either want to seek revenge or give it to God. You either want this wound healed or open to drain energy and life from you. It is your choice.

Your answer could be yes because you remember the exact date and time you forgave. However, suppose you let your bad thinking and emotions control you, resulting in using the offense against them. In that case, you are still "paying attention to" or have "marked" the location of the "weapon" and have started using it again. The solution is to go back and forgive. It would also help to confess to the Lord and the other person that you have sinned against them for letting bitterness and revenge control you.

Finally, your answer could be yes, but you continue to think about what happened. Your thoughts are not toward revenge or bitterness; you remember it and the pain of going through that event. Do these three things.

1. Use the power of 2 Corinthians 10:4-5. The end of verse 5 says, "bringing every thought into captivity to the obedience of Christ."

2. Hand the thoughts to Jesus Christ, saying, "Lord, I know that I forgave, that I didn't lie about the forgiveness, and You know I did not lie. You deal with the thoughts and remove them from me."

3. Move quickly to step seven.

As you continue to subject those thoughts to Christ, you will struggle with them less, and the wound will heal.

Step Seven—Enjoy Freedom & Healing

If you have not forgiven, it will be extremely hard to do what this step requires. If you have forgiven, this step speeds the healing.

Louie (my wife) had a severe break in her left arm at the elbow that required a metal plate and screws to give her use of the arm again. Not long after the surgery, the doctor prescribed working with a physical therapist to rebuild the muscles and maximize the flexibility of her elbow. That therapy was not fun, it was painful, but it was necessary to maximize the healing and use of her arm.

Step Seven is like working with a therapist. What you are asked to do may not be easy, but it is imperative if you want freedom and healing. This step requires the following:

- Praying for God's blessing upon them.
- Encouraging them.
- Pursuing their best by finding ways to serve them.

When you come through step six and verify that you have forgiven, this step will help you continue moving forward. Without this last step, it will be easy to let the memory of the pain of what they did to you pull you back toward vengeance and bitterness. You will find immense power in this step.

You may be mumbling something like, "You have got to be kidding! You are asking me to not only let the offense go, but now you are asking me to pray blessing upon them?" Yes, I am because it is what Christ did. This step follows the marvelous example of Jesus Christ.

We participated with the people of Jerusalem in the crucifixion of Jesus. He was beaten and tortured, then hung on the cross. As Jesus was on the cross, He asked His Father to forgive us and the people of Jerusalem.

He then died, rose again, and appeared to many people. Then He did something we want to imitate.

> *And being assembled together with them, He*
> *commanded them not to depart from Jerusalem,*
> *but to wait for the Promise of the Father,*
> *"which," He said, "you have heard from Me…*
> *But you shall receive power when the Holy Spirit*
> *has come upon you; and you shall be witnesses to*
> *Me in Jerusalem, and in all Judea and Samaria,*
> *and to the end of the earth.*

Acts 1:4, 8, NKJV

Jesus sent the Holy Spirit to the disciples to bless Jerusalem, the very people who did Him wrong! Blessing people who have harmed you is impossible without forgiveness. Until we, too, forgive those who have wronged us, we cannot pray God's blessing upon them, encourage them, or pursue their best. And until we do so, we will not experience the freedom and healing God wants for us.

Ensure your healing! Pray for them, bless them, and find ways to pursue their best. Enjoy the Freedom!

REFLECTIVE QUESTIONS

- Do you find it difficult to remember that forgiveness pleases God? Meditate on Ephesians 4:32. Make a note of how meditating on that scripture impacts your attitude.

  _____

  _____

  _____

- Who do you need to forgive? What will be the result in terms of freedom when you truly forgive them?

  _____

  _____

  _____

- Has unforgiveness robbed your joy? Imagine what it would be like to have your joy back. Determine who you need to forgive and start the process.

  _____

  _____

  _____

  _____

- If you are having trouble forgiving someone, or keep thinking about what happened, ask yourself if you are Flashing your ME. What can you do to change your mindset or thinking to quiet the Flashing ME?

_____

_____

_____

_____

SUBMISSION, AUTHORITY AND LEADERSHIP

The book titled *The S Word* from this book series provides an in-depth look at submission and how it impacts your relationship with God and others. It is such a huge part of the solution for GR8 Relationships that we have included it in this book as well.

Left to your sin nature, you will constantly want to be in control, or to be in charge. You are not being submissive, but more likely telling, or wanting to tell, people what to do. Obviously, that is not how submission works. Submission helps you pursue the best for others. It is the component of relationships where you serve others. To understand why this is true, you need a good definition of submission.

When you look at the Greek word *hupotássō,* which translates to submit, it means the following.

- To place in order
- To place under in an orderly fashion

When used in Ephesians 5:22, it is *hupotássomai,* which further means

- To subject oneself
- Place oneself in submission

It is a choice to yield to another person. The military provides a clear picture of what the word means. The military has officers and those *under* the officers, or commanders and the people under the commanders. And the officers or commanders are under the ultimate leader.

The non-military usage is similar. Consider the hierarchy in your job or in an organization. You may be a training professional in your company. People may report to you, but you have a boss who has a boss. If all of you were just doing your own thing, it would be chaos. Being part of a team and ultimately part of a company department, you have someone to submit to. This doesn't mean you just blindly do what you are told to do especially if it violates God's Word. However, you yield yourself to the authority or will of another because you want to align with your organization and the team you are a part of in that organization. So, submission means to line up underneath. Why? For *order,* or to create order. Think about how that might work in your current work situation.

When you are in a relationship and following this idea of submission, you are willing to line yourself up underneath another person to support them and maintain order. This is not all there is to submission, but it is a critical use of submission.

Notice how this works with love. When you pursue their best patiently, kindly, sacrificially, and unconditionally you willingly line up underneath them. All of God's Word fits together, and this is just one piece of what makes relationships work best.

Please keep in mind that submission is for everyone, not just for women! Remember Ephesians 5:21 states, "Submitting yourselves one to another."

So, men, please, never talk to your wife about submission if you do not understand it yourself. Until you learn how to submit to your boss the way God wants you to and submit to authorities the way God wants you to, please do not try to get anyone to submit to you, much less your wife.

A simple, workable definition of submission is:

---

*An internal, voluntary act of the will
to yield to another.*

You choose to submit. No one can make you submit.

Here are four Bible verses that provide the practical application of submission in your daily life.

. . . that you also submit to such, and to everyone who works and labors with us.

1 Corinthians 16:16, NKJV

Therefore submit yourselves to every ordinance of man for the Lord's sake, whether to the king as supreme, or to governors, as to those who are sent by him for the punishment of evildoers and for the praise of those who do good.

1 Peter 2:13-14, NKJV

Likewise you younger people, submit yourselves to your elders. Yes, all of you be submissive to one another, and be clothed with humility, for "God resists the proud, but gives grace to the humble.

1 Peter 5:5, NKJV

Obey those who rule over you, and be submissive, for they watch out for your souls, as those who must give account. Let them do so with joy and not with grief, for that would be unprofitable for you.

Hebrews 13:17, NKJV

Many other scriptures are just as clear and practical. They can impact daily life. God's Word clearly wants you to submit. Why? Because this is the way the body of Christ works best. God wants each member of the body serving the others, thinking of others as more important than themselves rather than their *ME* flashing all the time. God wants you to submit to others in the fear of God, because that makes the body healthy.

Submission Displays God's Image

Submission is actually displayed between the Father, Son, and the Holy Spirit. Let's look at submission with regard to the image of God. What could be a more important topic than the image of God?

When you apply the image of God to what you study in the Bible, you gain new insight into that area of study. As you study submission, two approaches tend to show up. One is authority and submission, and the other is mutual submission. Authority and submission might be obvious. It is the powerful element of the image of God. Mutual submission is the relational aspect of the image of God.

Submission is a word that describes how people relate to each other, but every relationship has a power element and relating element. For submission, the authority and submission approach concerns *order* in the relationship. On the other hand, the mutual submission approach provides the *harmony*, or relating aspect of the relationship.

You reduce chaos in the relationship when you have order, and you reduce the flashing *ME* in a relationship when you have harmony. Order is an impersonal structure, and harmony is a personal structure.

The problem with discussing submission is people only want to talk about one side or the other. Mostly, people want to talk about mutual submission. They only want to talk about how we are supposed to be mutually submitting one to another in the fear of God.

The relational side of submission is definitely important; however, the power, order, or authority and submission attribute is equally important. Both must be considered because Christians are supposed to voluntarily put themselves under authority (to maintain order) and carry the burdens for others (to enhance the relationship). When you do it that way, with order and harmony, you practice submission in a way that fits the image of God.

Submission Displays the Mind of Christ

It is easy to shy away from (or ignore) submission, so we call it the *S Word*. People do not want to discuss submission because it seems too controversial. And, of course, when it involves women to men or wife to husband, "Oh, don't touch that one! That's not politically correct!"

This powerful word has such a bad reputation, even though it plugs directly into the solution for every relationship. The minute you submit the way God wants you to, it not only demonstrates the mind of Christ, but it also completely cancels out the *Flashing ME*.

The mind of Jesus Christ is clearly shown in the scripture below from Philippians.

> *Let nothing be done through selfish ambition or conceit, but in lowliness of mind let each esteem others better than himself. Let each of you look out not only for his own interests, but also for the interests of others. Let this mind be in you which was also in Christ Jesus, who, being in the form of God, did not consider it robbery to be equal with God, but made Himself of no reputation, taking the form of a bondservant, and coming in the likeness of men. And being found in appearance as a man, He humbled Himself and became obedient to the point of death, even the death of the cross.*

Philippians 2:3-8, NKJV

When you have the mind of Christ, you think of others as more important than yourself. You put their interests in front of yours, as seen in verses three and four. You can see in verses five through eight that the mind of Christ lowers you to sacrifice for others and submit to the needs of others. That is precisely how Christ wants you to think about relationships.

Christ submitted to our needs. Christ has all authority. Everything lines up underneath Him. He is the authority. He provides the *order* for the entire universe. He is in charge, but notice what He did.

He took His authority and said, "I'm going to create harmony between you and Me. I have all authority. I can order anything to be the way I want it, so I am going to provide the path for you to have *harmony* with Me." So you can see the two elements of submission in those verses.

Submission is always voluntary for both order and harmony. You voluntarily line yourself underneath someone to support them, even if you are the leader, and you focus on whether they are lining up underneath you. When you lead, you use both elements of submission to create both order and harmony. When you submit in this way, you demonstrate love and pursue their best patiently, kindly, sacrificially, and unconditionally.

If you do not have the foundation of love, submission will be exceedingly difficult. So, I believe love comes first. It is the highest of all the values. And when you submit with the correct intent of your heart, you practice the love of God with others.

Mutual Submission

Submission is a component of all healthy relationships. The easiest one to apply to is marriage, but it also applies to work, friendship, and family relationships. Applied correctly in marriages, submission provides order and establishes harmony between husband and wife. Unfortunately, many people use submission in marriage toward women more than men, which implies they focus on order and not harmony.

The apostle Paul speaks of how submission and love apply to various relationships, as listed below.

- Ephesians 5:21: Mutual submission as the standard for all believers:

submitting to one another in the fear of God

Ephesians 5:21, NKJV

- The passage that follows, Ephesians 5:22-31, mutual submission and love is the standard for the marriage:

Wives, submit to your own husbands, as to the Lord. For the husband is head of the wife, as also Christ is head of the church; and He is the Savior of the body. Therefore, just as the church is subject to Christ, so let the wives be to their own husbands in everything.

Husbands, love your wives, just as Christ also
loved the church and gave Himself for her, that
He might [a]sanctify and cleanse her with the
washing of water by the word, that He might
present her to Himself a glorious church, not
having spot or wrinkle or any such thing, but
that she should be holy and without blemish. So
husbands ought to love their own wives as
their own bodies; he who loves his wife loves
himself. For no one ever hated his own flesh,
but nourishes and cherishes it, just as the
Lord does the church. For we are members of His
body, [b]of His flesh and of His bones. "For this
reason a man shall leave his father and mother
and be joined to his wife, and the two shall
become one flesh.

Ephesians 5:22-31

- Continuing through Ephesians 6:1-4,
  mutual submission is for parents and
  children (the family):

Children, obey your parents in the Lord, for this
is right. "Honor your father and mother," which
is the first commandment with promise: "that
it may be well with you and you may live long
on the earth." And you, fathers, do not provoke

your children to wrath, but bring them up in the
training and admonition of the Lord

Ephesians 6:1-4, NKJV

- And in Ephesians 6:5-9, mutual submission applies to the workplace:

Bondservants, be obedient to those who are your
masters according to the flesh, with fear and
trembling, in sincerity of heart, as to Christ;
not with eyeservice, as men-pleasers, but as
bondservants of Christ, doing the will of God
from the heart, with goodwill doing service,
as to the Lord, and not to men, knowing that
whatever good anyone does, he will receive the
same from the Lord, whether he is a slave or free.

And you, masters, do the same things to them,
giving up threatening, knowing that [a]your
own Master also is in heaven, and there is no
partiality with Him.

Ephesians 6:5-9, NKJV

Submission and Authority

One of the reasons people struggle with submission and authority is that they look at the world's view of this topic. God's view of authority and leadership differs from what many people think. Our savior Jesus Christ taught his disciples a different idea of authority and leadership.

> *Jesus called them together and said, "you know that the rulers of the Gentiles lord it over them, and their high officials exercise authority over them. Not so with you. Instead whoever wants to become great among you must be your servant, and whoever wants to be first must be your slave—just as the Son of Man did not come to be served, but to serve, and to give his life as ransom for many."*

Matthew 20:25-28, NIV

Jesus Christ did not come to be served; He came to serve. He is a perfect example of what *servants leading servants* means. Most leadership focuses on control. The Pharisees thought that way. The Gentile lords, kings, world leaders, and presidents of countries and businesses have adopted that view of authority and leadership.

Looking at our society today, you can see plenty of examples of this viewpoint: Do you want to be a great leader? You must have money and power! The more money and power you have, the larger your control and the stronger you will become.

The world celebrates men of power, fame, and money, so that temptation will always be close to you when you are a leader or are influential. You will be tempted to make things go your way. You will be tempted to get people to serve you. You will be tempted to get money from people inappropriately, especially in a church.

Do you want to be great in the eyes of men, or great in God's eyes? So, how will you know if you are a godly leader? Is it because men and women say so? Is it the size of your church or organization, or how big your budget is? How many people attend or the size of your staff.

You may assume you are a good leader because you are a religious leader. Be cautious because that was the mistake of the Pharisees and scribes, the religious leaders of the day during Jesus Christ's time.

> *Beware of the scribes, who desire to go around in long robes, love greetings in marketplaces, the best seats in the synagogues, and the best places at feasts, who devour widows' houses, and for a pretense make long prayers. These will receive their condemnation.*

Luke 20:46-47

If you are trying to draw attention to the success *you* created as a religious leader, your mind needs a reset and renewal. That is not what God wants, and it is not godly thinking. Jesus was the original Servant Leader, as described above in Matthew 20:25-28.

Ask God to renew your mind to be a Servant Leader under Jesus Christ's authority. When you see authority and leadership the way God does, your thinking and view changes. Your transformation into the leader God wants you to be has begun.

Godly Authority Encourages Freedom

Unfortunately, authority is often misused. When people think of or use *their* authority, they may do one of the following:
- Demand justification or evidence.
- State that a person has expert abilities and knowledge.
- Demonstrate power to decide.
- Grant freedom for others to act.

While the above are basically positive, do they fit your definition of authority? Do you have a favorable view and behavior when you wield authority?

For most people, the answer is no. Authority is constantly misused and creates an image of harshness or abuse. It is also misused when seen as a person— meaning the person in charge. Finally, it is misused when the person with the authority minimizes everyone's freedom except their own.

Most dictators around the world misuse the authority God has given them and assume they are the authority. But they, like you, are not the authority. You, like Paul, are only a channel or steward of the authority given by God.

> *Let every soul be subject to the governing authorities. For there is no authority except from God, and the authorities that exist are appointed by God.*

Romans 13:1, NKJV

As a leader, you are only a channel of authority, a steward of the authority God has given to you. God is the ultimate authority over everything, and He uses good and bad people as channels of His authority in the world.

Let's define authority, understand how God sees authority, and look at the biblical example of the Apostle Paul as a channel of God's authority.

The Greek word for authority is *exousia*, which indicates "freedom of choice." So, a person with great authority has the maximum freedom of choice. On the other hand, the one under the authority most often has limited freedom. That is the way it works in the world, but that is not the way God wants you to use His authority. You are His channel of authority.

Since God is the only authority, it is wise to see how He used His authority with us. Here's what Galatians says:

*Stand fast therefore in the liberty by which Christ
has made us free, and do not be entangled again
with a yoke of bondage.*

Galatians 5:1, NKJV

God used His authority through the death of Jesus
Christ the Son to set us *free*! That means God's example
for us as channels of His authority is to use it to provide
freedom, not control.

This means authority is definitely not about *ME*.
It is not about your position or power. Using authority
as God intended means encouraging, even creating,
freedom of choice for those you lead and others around
you. It does not mean there are no boundaries or
consequences for people who do not follow the rules.
Authority appropriately used allows people to cross the
boundaries and experience the consequences, the same
way God deals with you.

Are you using God's authority correctly by
enhancing freedom rather than restricting it? If so, you
can become an even better leader when you are gentle
and willing to serve those under and around you. This
allows you to trust God's power to direct and deal with
people.

You can see more about leadership in our book
*Servants Leading Servants – 15 Signs of a Real Servant
Leader.*

PERSONAL TRANSFORMATION

P ersonal transformation for the better creates a long-term change in someone that will always impact relationships no matter their context. 2 Peter gives us clarity of what God has done and is willing to do through us, what He wants us to do, and what He promises if we do it:

> But also for this very reason, giving all diligence,
> add to your faith virtue, to virtue knowledge,
> to knowledge self-control, to self-control
> perseverance, to perseverance godliness, to
> godliness brotherly kindness, and to brotherly
> kindness love. For if these things are yours
> and abound, you will be neither barren nor
> unfruitful in the knowledge of our Lord
> Jesus Christ. For he who lacks these things is
> shortsighted, even to blindness, and has forgotten
> that he was cleansed from his old sins.

2 Peter 1:5-9, NKJV

Steps to Transformation

Peter provides three key terms at the beginning of verse 5. These are especially important because they set the stage for the eight steps.

"For this very reason . . . " While observing this verse, you may have asked, "What reason is Peter referring to?" The answer is in the previous verses. Peter stated that God provided you "exceeding great and precious promises," gifted you "all things pertaining to life and godliness," allows you to be "partakers of the divine nature," so you may escape "the corruption in the world through lust." Remember all that? Any one of those four is "reason" enough to do what Peter is about to ask you to do. God's provision means you are thoroughly equipped for what follows, thoroughly equipped for transformation!

". . . giving all diligence . . . " A standard issue raised by Bible scholars relates to God's control of all things and mankind's ability to freely choose. Much energy is put into these discussions trying to either reconcile them or determine how one should be emphasized over the other. The issue is worthy of your consideration and this passage makes those discussions relevant.

How much of this transformation is God's job and how much is yours? This phrase clearly states your responsibility to choose. On the other hand, the Holy Spirit enables you to fulfill your choice. Transformation requires diligence to trust in the power of God in you, discipline to choose that power, and focus on what God says in His Word.

"...add to..." Not only are you asked to be diligent, but the Greek word translated as "add to" is packed with additional meaning. The verb *epichorēgein* comes from the noun *chorēgos*, which literally means the leader of a chorus. Perhaps the greatest gift that Greece, and especially Athens, gave to the world was the great works of men like Aeschylus, Sophocles, and Euripides, which are still among its most cherished possessions. All these plays needed large choruses and were, therefore, very expensive to produce. In the great days of Athens there were public-spirited citizens who voluntarily took on the duty, at their own expense, of collecting, maintaining, training, and equipping such choruses. Men had to be found to provide the choruses, a duty which could cost as much as 3,000 drachmae. The men who undertook these duties out of their own pocket and out of love for their city were called *chorēgoi*, and *chorēgein* was the verb used for undertaking such a duty. The word has a certain lavishness in it. It never means to equip in any cheese-paring and miserly way; it means lavishly to pour out everything necessary for a noble performance. *Epichorēgein* went out into a larger world and it grew to mean not only to equip a chorus but to be responsible for any kind of equipment. It can mean to equip an army with all necessary provisions. It can mean to equip the soul with all the necessary virtues for life. But always at the back of it there is this idea of a lavish generosity in the equipment. (*The letters of James and Peter. 2000 (W. Barclay, lecturer in the University of Glasgow, Ed.). The Daily study Bible series, Rev. ed. (298–299). Philadelphia: The Westminster Press.)*

Peter is *urging you* to equip your life with every virtue, and equipping is not simply a necessary minimum, but lavish and generous. You are asked to be content with nothing less than the loveliest and the most splendid life.

You can furnish, supply, and support lavishly each step of this transformation. Think of putting on a party with your best dishes, decorations, and food. Think of a runner going that extra mile, doing the extra repetition in the weight room, or eating only the best diet in preparation for an important race.

Whatever is needed, DO IT!

Step One—Faith

Faith is the first step in your transformation. Faith is adequately defined as a "Firm persuasion, a conviction based upon hearing." God has provided us with the ability to have this "firm persuasion." Let's look at 2 Peter to see something unique about faith:

> *Simon Peter, a bondservant and apostle of Jesus*
> *Christ, To those who have obtained like precious*

*faith with us by the righteousness of our God and
Savior Jesus Christ.*

2 Peter 1:1, NKJV

The word *obtained* refers to how we got our faith,
and it tends to give a wrong impression of what the
Greek word means. The Greek-English Lexicon of the
New Testament (*Louw-Nida*) provides the definition
below:

*To receive, with the implication that the process is
related somehow to divine will or favor.*

So, this faith is not something you searched for,
selected, or purchased. It is something God gave you
because of His marvelous character and grace.

It is the same faith given to the apostles.

So, what is this faith? I believe it is Jesus' death,
burial, and resurrection,

*So then faith comes by hearing and hearing by
the word of God.*

Romans 10:17, NKJV

Your transformation process starts with faith in
Jesus! Without Him, you have little power to do any
of the following seven steps. This faith is a ". . . like
precious faith with us," which means like the apostles.
While I am not at the same level as the apostles, I am
in the same family. And they, like you and me, can have

a "like precious faith" when we accept the reality of the death, burial, and resurrection of Jesus Christ.

The transformation process will not work unless God in His power is working in you and you are choosing to do what He asks. Because God is so gracious, He provides what you need to get started: FAITH! Also, He provides what you need to keep going, the life of Jesus and the energy of His Spirit. Faith is also tied to humility. You have more opportunity to trust God when you accept you are under God. Humility accepts the fact you can't and won't change without God's provision.

> *But without faith it is impossible to please Him,*
> *for he who comes to God must believe that He is,*
> *and that He is a rewarder of those who diligently*
> *seek Him.*

Hebrews 11:6, NKJV

Step Two—Virtue, Goodness, Moral Excellence

Do you want the virtues, goodness, or moral excellence of Jesus Christ?

This step is about you saying to God, "I recognize you are the Lord, the Master, and I am the servant. I accept my place. I want to be like You and what You want me to be."

Using the faith God has provided, you can now trust His ability to conform you into the image of His Son, Jesus Christ.

The Greek word for virtue denotes valor and excellence. There's nothing soft or weak about virtue. When virtues are assimilated into your life, they allow you to fulfill your real purpose in life, becoming like Christ to glorify God. Consider some key virtues of Jesus Christ.

The fruit of the Spirit is love, joy, peace, patience, kindness, goodness, faithfulness, gentleness, and self-control.

In the Sermon on the Mount, Jesus talks about the value of humility, dependence on God, gentleness, meekness, a desire for personal righteousness, mercy, purity of heart (inward cleanness), being a peacemaker, and accepting persecution.

If you are more proud than humble in your thinking, then you will not likely accept the opportunity to become more like Christ, adopting His virtues. Hopefully, that is not true of you. Hopefully, you desire to be transformed by focusing on one virtue at a time.

Step Three—Knowledge

This refers to spiritual knowledge, knowledge about the virtue or moral excellence that you would like in your life. It is the "practical knowledge" of learning from God how things work, how to handle life successfully. It is an understanding of life drawn from God's Word, which includes practical discrimination of good and evil, and intelligent appreciation of what the will of God is in your daily activities.

This knowledge comes from God, primarily through God's Word. It is not knowledge for just knowing something, but for transformation and being conformed into being like Christ Jesus. The more you learn about the virtues of Jesus Christ, it is likely that you will desire to have those virtues in your life.

Spiritual knowledge can deepen your desire and need for transformation, but that is not causal. It is still your choice to use it. Knowledge helps change your thinking, preparing you for self-control or temperance, the next step.

Step Four—Self-Control

Self-control is the ability to *hold yourself in*, have your passions under control, reining in your improper desires and lusts. Probably the best way to get self-control into your thinking is to reverse the words to *control self*. That's what this is about. Control of self is critical to your ability to make sense of life and operate in life in a manner that pleases God.

> *He who is slow to anger is better than the mighty,*
> *and he who rules his spirit than he who takes a city.*

Proverbs 16:32, NKJV

> *Whoever has no rule over his own spirit is like a*
> *city broken down, without walls.*

Proverbs 25:28, NKJV

Unfortunately, many believe self-control is something that is solely their responsibility, therefore, they must "get it done."

But you are battling with your sin nature and self-control or control of self is a fruit of the Spirit. You only achieve control of self with the energy and power of the Holy Spirit. That is such a simple thought, but so important. Please do not miss that the Spirit wars against the flesh, not you. You cannot win that battle; only God can.

Step Five—Perseverance

You want to change or transformation, so you trust in God's provision (the life of Christ and the Holy Spirit), decide to seek at least one of the virtues or values of Jesus Christ, learn about it, and begin to apply it to your life so that it will control self.

Now it becomes even more important to realize how much this depends on the energy and power of the Holy Spirit, because sticking with your choice is often difficult. You need perseverance to stay the course.

Perseverance is constant and steadfast endurance under adversity, with no giving in or giving up. Think about a balancing mobile like the one hanging above a baby's crib. If that mobile could talk, it would tell you its primary desire is to be stationary, stable, and in equilibrium.

Your life and relationships are like that mobile, desiring stability and sameness rather than change. Even if the change is good, the "mobile" does not want it because it means that it will no longer be stable. If you are one piece of that mobile and you want to move to a different location, the whole mobile has to move to adjust to your new position. Does the mobile or system just accept your movement? Not likely! It will do what it can to force you to return to where you were because it wants stability, not movement.

There is good news and bad news here. The good news is you have decided to be transformed. The bad news is your system will work against that change.

Now do you see how important the power of the Holy Spirit is in this process?

This part of the process requires both your choice and your trust in the energy of the Holy Spirit to continue the transformation.

> *And not grow weary while doing good, for in due season we shall reap if we do not lose heart.*

Galatians 6:9, NKJV

> *And not only that, but we also glory in tribulations, knowing that tribulation produces perseverance; and perseverance, character; and character, hope.*

Romans 5:3-4, NKJV

My brethren, count it all joy when you fall into various trials, knowing that the testing of your faith produces patience.

James 1:2-3, NKJV

Indeed we count them blessed who endure. You have heard of the perseverance of Job and seen the end intended by the Lord—that the Lord is very compassionate and merciful.

James 5:1, NKJV

Step Six—Godliness

This is the best definition of godliness I have found:

. . . lives above the petty things of life, the passions and pressures that control the lives of others. He seeks to do the will of God and, as he does, he seeks the welfare of others…He does what is right because it is right and because it is the will of God.

Warren Wiersbe, Bible Exposition Commentary

Stop and reflect on what he is saying. Godliness lives above the petty issues of life. That means, because of your humanity, you will see what is happening to you according to human eyes. You will see things from an earthly, human perspective, not God's.

As you move through these steps, faith, virtue, knowledge, self-control, then perseverance, the next step in your transformation is beginning to see life differently. Things that were once a big deal are now seen for what they really are: temporal and petty. Your ME flashing made something big out of something petty.

Now with new eyes, you see some of life through God's perspective, doing what is right, not because you expect a return, but because, according to God, it is the right thing to do. Godliness has an exceptional practical value for you, because this is where you begin participating in the divine nature of God, benefitting from the exceeding great and precious promises, and escaping the corruption in this world. Let's look at the scriptures regarding this.

> *But reject profane and old wives' fables, and exercise yourself toward godliness. For bodily exercise profits a little, but godliness is profitable for all things, having promise of the life that now is and of that which is to come. This is a faithful saying and worthy of all acceptance.*

I Timothy 4:7-9, NKJV

> *Now godliness with contentment is great gain.*

I Timothy 6:6, NKJV

Seeing things through God's eyes plus accepting where you are and what you have as God's plan equals great gain. These steps for personal transformation provide real satisfaction and contentment. That is a great gain!

Step Seven—Brotherly Kindness

Godliness is the transition point from the internal part of the process to the external part. You have trusted in Jesus and His life in you, adopted a virtue, learned about it, applied it to yourself, persevered with it, and have begun to see life differently, through God's eyes, not your own, at least in this one small area.

Brotherly kindness is a fervent, practical care and concern for others' needs.

For relationships, the Problem is making everything about ME (flashing your ME). The Solution is pursuing their best patiently, kindly, sacrificially, and unconditionally.

This seventh step takes you toward the solution.

If someone says, "I love God," and hates his brother, he is a liar; for he who does not love his brother whom he has seen, how can he love God whom he has not seen?

I John 4:20, NKJV

Be kindly affectionate to one another with brotherly love, in honor giving preference to one another . . .

Romans 12:10, NKJV

We must add brotherly-kindness, a tender affection to all our fellow-Christians, who are children of the same Father, servants of the same Master, members of the same family, travelers to the same country, and heirs of the same inheritance, and therefore are to be loved with a pure heart fervently . . . as those who are peculiarly near and dear to us, in whom we take particular delight.

Matthew Henry, Bible Commentator

Dr. Marlin Howe stated you could always know you were being transformed when you begin to serve others through what God is teaching you. Those virtues you learned, applied, persevered with, and started seeing through God's eyes are now being worked out of your life into other's lives around you. This step is where you apply the below scripture.

. . . work out your own salvation with fear and trembling; for it is God who works in you both to will and to do for His good pleasure.

Philippians 2:12-13, NKJV

When you "work out your salvation," it is not that you are working for it, but that you are taking what God has done in you and using it for the benefit of others, therefore, working it out and moving from the inside to the outside.

Step Eight—Love

Love is the end-result God desires for every virtue that you, with His energy, assimilate into your life. That is the Solution for every relationship difficulty. No relationship will last without both parties using this solution, but you can only control applying the solution to your life.

Here again, is the working definition of love: Pursuing their best (highest good) patiently, kindly, sacrificially, and unconditionally.

Love is the final step of transformation, which indicates its importance. And indeed, it takes the transformation of a selfish, self-centered heart before there is any focus on pursuing the best for others.

The more virtues you learn about, apply, persevere with, see through God's eyes with, express to those around you, and finally pursue the best for anyone unconditionally, means you are being transformed into the beautiful image of your Lord and Savior Jesus Christ.

REFLECTIVE QUESTIONS

- Try rating yourself on how well you do on each virtue from the below lists. Where do you need to improve?

_____

_____

_____

- "The fruit of the Spirit is love, joy, peace, patience, kindness, goodness, faithfulness, gentleness, and self-control."

_____

_____

_____

- In the Sermon on the Mount, Jesus talks about the value of humility, dependence on God, gentleness, meekness, a desire for personal righteousness, mercy, purity of heart (inward cleanness), being a peacemaker, and accepting persecution.

_____

_____

_____

- What will be some of your challenges with personal transformation?

_____

_____

_____

_____

- What are the benefits of personal transformation to you and your relationships?

_____

_____

_____

_____

STUDY GUIDE

Scripture Meditation

Time: 30 minutes a day

Each day read and meditate on one of the scriptures listed below or as directed by your session leader.

Follow these steps.

1. Get in a quiet place without distraction.
2. Play a praise song, and just listen to the words.
3. Ask God to reveal His heart and meaning to you as you read the scriptures.
4. Write your reflections below or in your journal.
5. Read the scriptures daily so you receive maximum revelation.

I Corinthians 13: 4-8, NKJV	Matthew 22:37-40, NKJV	I John 4:20-21, NKJV
Romans 12:17, NKJV	Romans 8:28, NKJV	Acts 1:4, 8, NKJV
Philippians 2:3-8, NKJV	Ephesians 5:21, NKJV	Matthew 20:25-28, NIV
2 Peter 1:5-9, NKJV	Hebrews 11:6, NKJV	Proverbs 16:32, NKJV
I Timothy 4:7-9, NKJV	James 1:2-3, NKJV	Romans 5:3-4, NKJV
I John 4:20, NKJV	Romans 12:10, NKJV	Philippians 2:12-13, NKJV

REFLECTIVE QUESTIONS

- How can you apply principles of the Solution presented in this chapter to your relationship with your spouse, other family members, or co-workers?

  _____

  _____

  _____

- Thank about the working definition of Love. What new perspective did you learn about the definition of Love? How will applying what you learned improve your current relationships?

  _____

  _____

  _____

- What new insight did you gain about freedom? How will you apply that to your life and relationships?

  _____

  _____

  _____

  _____

- Think about the expectations you have for your spouse or significant other. First, write a few of them down, then determine whether they are hurting or helping your relationship. If they are hurting the relationship, what can you do to change them?

_____

_____

_____

- How can you apply forgiveness to relationships with your spouse, significant other, children, or co-workers? What do you need to change? What impact do you think that would have in the relationship?

_____

_____

_____

_____

- What personal actions do you need to take within the eight steps of Personal Transformation?

_____

_____

_____

_____

TOOLS

Each book in this series has a supplemental video course on www.gr8relate.com/video-courses/ under the heading "BOOK SERIES Video Courses." The videos were selected from the COMPLETE Video Courses to support the book and provide more details. If you want more details than the book offers, use the COMPLETE Video Courses and the GR8 Relationships Study Guide.

The following tools will enable you to understand yourself and your spouse and how you can work together to handle conflict. The videos listed below are a part of the video course that corresponds to the information in this book. Completing all the courses will be instrumental in helping you find FREEDOM!

You can find all these tools and many more on our website, www.gr8relate.com, on the TOOLS tab.

Kolbe Assessment https://gr8relate.com/kolbe

You can trust the validity and accuracy of the Kolbe instrument to show you your strengths and instincts. The Kolbe also helps you easily see and understand how the strengths and talents of one person may not be considered as strengths by another. This critical information will help you bridge the gap between reality and your expectations of them. Once you complete the assessment, you will receive detailed reports that will help you understand your strengths and talents and how to use your strengths in a complementary way with your spouse, family member, or friend's strengths. By understanding your instincts, you can more easily discuss your differences, laugh about them and develop ways to deal with them.

The Thomas-Kilman Conflict Mode Instrument (TKI) https://gr8relate.com/tki

The TKI is the world's best-selling instrument for understanding conflict. It helps you see that conflict can be beneficial and useful instead of thinking conflict as bad. You will be provided detailed information on effectively using all five conflict modes—competing, collaborating, compromising, avoiding, and accommodating.

The Fundamental Interpersonal Relations Orientation-Behavior™ (FIRO-B®). https://gr8relate.com/firob

The FIRO-B helps you understand how you interact at work and personal life. This easy-to-complete assessment will provide critical insights into how an individual interacts with others. This personality instrument measures how you typically behave with others and how you expect them to act toward you.

Individual Videos

We have a FREE video course that corresponds with the information in this book._

These are short courses that you can watch/listen at your own pace. Enter the information in parenthesis below into your browser and you will be taken to a video course. When you are online, scroll down and click the "Sign Up / Start Course" button to create an account. You only need an account to access all the free courses.

There are two options:

- BOOK SERIES Courses: Each book in the GR8 Relationships series will have a video course with specific videos selected from the COMPLETE Courses that help explain the contents of the book. This book's video course is below.
  - *The Solution (https://gr8relate.com/ video-courses/the-solution/)*
- COMPLETE Courses: These are the original, complete courses that give you more details about the information in this book.

- *07A – The Solution for Great Relationships (https://gr8relate. com/video-courses/solution-for- great-relationships/)*
- *07B - The Solution's Ingredients (https://gr8relate.com/video- courses/solutions-ingredients/)*
- *08A – Freedom from Being Emotion Led (https://gr8relate.com/video- courses/freedom-from-being- emotion-led/)*
- *08B – Freedom and Choice Is an Amazing Lifestyle (https://gr8relate. com/video-courses/freedom-and- choice-is-an-amazing-lifestyle/)*
- *08C – Freedom from Bitterness, Resentments, and Grudges (https://gr8relate.com/video- courses/freedom-from-bitterness- resentments-and-grudges/)*
- *09A – The "S" Word – Submission (https://gr8relate.com/video- courses/s-word-submission/)*
- *09B – Authority and Leadership – Paul's Example (https://gr8relate. com/video-courses/authority-and- leadership-pauls-example/)*
- *10 – The Solution Transforms (https://gr8relate.com/video- courses/solution-transforms/)*

Love's Current Reality

	Score yourself on how you relate to your SPOUSE or a SPECIAL relationship. Use a 1 to 10 scale, where 1 is worst, and 10 is best (10 = Never or Always in the statements below)	
1.	I suffer long; I am patient— I always endure evil, injury, and provocation, without being filled with resentment, bitterness, or grudges	
2.	I am kind—I always am gracious toward and do good for others	
3.	I do not envy, I am not jealous—I never compare myself to others, never suspect unfaithfulness, never feel inferior because of comparison	
4.	I do not brag or boast—I never have an "I" problem, never judge or act like I am better than others	
5.	I am not puffed up, proud—I never call attention to myself, never puffed up about myself or my possessions	
6.	I do not behave rudely—I am always courteous, respectful, considerate, chivalrous, gallant	
7.	I do not seek my own—I am never self-seeking or self-absorbed, never have to have it my way	
8.	I am not provoked—I am never easily angered or react to what others are doing to me, always operate on Godly values	
9.	I think no evil—I never keep a list or think of wrongs done to me	
10.	I do not rejoice in evil—I never condone or tolerate evil or wrongdoing and never rejoice when it happens	
11.	I rejoice in truth—I am always delighted to see truth win, delighted when truth is shared with me when I have been wrong, delighted to get constructive criticism	
12.	I bear all things—I always protect others, never share their faults when speaking to others	
13.	I believe all things—I always trust, never suspicious, assuming, or reluctant to believe the best about others	
14.	I hope all things—I always hope for the best without controlling or manipulating	
15.	I endure all things—I always persevere in good and tough times, and I never feel compelled to talk about my problems	

Using the above information, identify 1 or 2 items you would like to enhance. Write an action you could regularly take this month to help you score higher next time.

Ten Steps to Your Best Relationships!

Do you desire to have better, healthier relationships? Do you find that on some days, it seems like a struggle? If so, you are not alone. Here are ten steps that can lead you to experience your best relationships ever.

Step 1. Study God's Design for Excellent Relationships

The design of a butter knife lets you know that it works best when spreading soft things like room-temperature butter. If you try to use it to cut a T-bone steak, you will see that it is not designed to do that. The same is true for excellent relationships.

God had a clear purpose and design when He created man and woman. He designed man to be different from a woman so that the two would not only be complimentary but, more importantly, display His image to a lost and dying world.

Step 2. Recognize How Men and Women Are Different - REALLY!

God created man and woman perfectly to fulfill their designed roles which complement each other.

If you remember, God created Eve because He did not want Adam alone. Without a woman, man has no one to help "fill the earth and subdue it" (Gen 1:28). Adam needed a suitable helper to fulfill God's purpose for mankind. And for a woman, it is imperative to remember that Helper is a word used primarily about God (i.e., Ps 121:1-2), further elevating rather than demeaning women.

God designed a woman to fulfill a relational role while a man fulfills his work role design – the differences are complementary, not conflicting.

Step 3. Accept the ONE PROBLEM!

Did you know that there is only ONE PROBLEM?

Making everything about ME is THE PROBLEM that destroys relationships. It is the root from which relationship mistakes grow. Unfortunately, we are blind to how often we make life about ME! You may have noticed how easy it is to see when others are being selfish and self-absorbed, but not when you are doing it.

When others are making life about ME, it's like they have this big ME on their forehead. They cannot see it – because it is on their forehead above their eyes! The same is true for you; they see it!

Step 4. Discover the Unknown Judgments for Men and Women

Every woman and man that has, is, and will live is subject to the judgments issued by God. And this affects every relationship.

Understanding these judgments is like unlocking the secrets of what drives and motivates lousy relationships. Learning these profound judgments enables you to identify difficulties and issues in your relationships and see the damage they are creating for you now.

Woman

- **Designed to RELATE:** The woman's unique design helps, nurtures, and supports healthy relationships, especially with her husband and children.
- **RELATING is Judged:** The woman's judgment adds pain to relationships and drives her to control them, which creates more pain, especially with her husband and children.

Man

- **Designed to WORK:** The man's design provides, protects, and preserves others, especially his wife and children.
- **WORK is Judged:** The man's judgment adds pain to work and drives him to control work, which creates more pain, especially for his wife and children.

Step 5. Devote Yourself to the SOLUTION

Would you be happy, or at least more satisfied, if they just changed?

That thinking encourages the PROBLEM, not the SOLUTION. You ignore the changes needed in your life because, after all, "They are the problem, not me..."

The Solution is the opposite of the Problem. The Solution will *pursue their best patiently, kindly, sacrificially, and unconditionally*. That is a definition of love from God's Word. God asks us to have "lowliness of mind to let each esteem others better than himself." (Phil 2:3)

When you live that definition, you relate to others as God relates to us. So, spend energy making changes *God wants you to make* and release the other person to God.

Love does not focus on ME or judge or complain about people, especially those near you. Love does not try to get others to help you change difficult people. Love never manipulates or dominates others to make you feel better. Instead, love always promises, promotes, and provides freedom for others to relate to you or not because it focuses on the best for others.

Step 6. Learn How Your Feelings Work

Great relationships depend on effectively understanding the link between thinking, feeling, acting, and the Solution. If you do not see how your emotions are always responding and are often untrustworthy, then you will not see how it can be dangerous to "follow your heart."

Please understand emotions or feelings are not bad, and you must become emotionless—quite the opposite. Your emotions are God-given but know that you can control them.

Step 7. Choose the Reality of Freedom

Freedom is "not controlling or being controlled." It dramatically changes relationships, yet it is not the most crucial element for superior relationships. Relationships will suffer from irresponsible freedom if freedom is not underneath the Solution. Choose wisely!

Remember, love is the Solution, and *pursues their best patiently, kindly, sacrificially, and unconditionally*. It takes your freedom to a higher standard, always responsible, never irresponsible (which limits your freedom). Love sets and respects boundaries; freedom without love is irresponsible and ignores boundaries. When your ME is flashing, it uses your freedom irresponsibly.

Step 8. Remove Bitterness, Resentment, and Grudges

Forgiveness removes bitterness, resentment, and grudges. It is the only way to get free from the harm others have done to you. Seriously, the only way!

It requires courage and trust in a PERFECT Father God to use it. There are severe consequences for you and your relationships when you do not forgive.

When you forgive, the result is freedom from being controlled by a past event or person that has harmed you.

Step 9. Confess. Deal with Real and False Guilt

Like forgiveness, superior relationships also need confession. Without those two, you have no cure for the pain of wrongs done to you and wrongs you do to others. Both are necessary to stop being controlled by the past.

Confession is how you deal with real guilt. It prevents you from being controlled by what you have done to others. It is an external act from an internal change of heart. And it is best done first to God, then to the person you harmed.

Because of Satan's constant bombardment of lies, he wants you to feel guilty for things God has not declared wrong. That is false guilt; one clear example occurs when you confess real guilt. Satan starts whispering in your ear, "But you still did it," trying to remove the freedom God grants (1 Jn 1:9). Yes, you did it, but God is no longer paying attention to it.

Step 10. Follow the Path to Transformation

God provided a clear path if you want transformation. God will not make you do the steps He has provided. But, when you start the process, you participate in the abundant life you have been given (2 Pet 1:3). The benefits and promises God states that are part of the abundant life are incredibly appealing. He says...

- you "...have been given...exceedingly great and precious promises" (2 Pet 1:3)
- that through the promises "you may be partakers of the divine nature" (2 Pet 1:4) and
- you have "escaped the corruption that is in this world" (2 Pet 1:4)

While that is incredible, He also reveals three promises if you take the transformation path and one painful, solemn warning if you don't (2 Pet 1:8-9). Start today practicing these steps for transformation.

Hermann Eben is the founder and CEO of GR8 Relationships. To know more, visit https://gr8relate.com/video-courses/). You will find FREE video courses that walk you through God's design. These courses are short and easy to follow and can put you on the path to Pursuing *Their* Best patiently, kindly, sacrificially, and unconditionally.

www.GR8Relate.com

51 Relationship Principles

1. Think of others as important, in fact, more important than you.

2. 3 Simple Guidelines; 3 Simple Questions
   a. Do what is right. Will I do what is right?
   b. Be trustworthy. Will I commit to doing my best?
   c. Do to others as you would have them do to you. Will I pursue the good of and serve others more than myself?

3. Freedom in relationships does not mean license; it primarily involves being a real person and letting others be themselves.

4. Freedom blossoms relationships: control and manipulation limit them.

5. Freedom in marriage allows each person to operate in their design.

6. If people are not free to be themselves around you, then, most likely, your relationships are all about YOU.

7. When freedom and choice are not in a relationship, someone is being controlled (dominated or manipulated).

8. When you cannot be yourself in a relationship, the relationship will become intolerable.

9. When freedom and choice are in a relationship, the whole person (good & bad) is accepted.

10. When you are tense, angry, frustrated, or irritated, it often means someone is not doing the job you assigned them.

11. Your happiness is a lousy job to assign to anyone or anything. Why let someone else control you that way?

12. When you take things personally, you are not operating in freedom.

13. Without freedom in a relationship, someone will be a fake, hypocrite, or liar.

14. If a relationship must satisfy you, you are walking down the manipulation trail (You are saying NO to the relationship and making the relationship about you; freedom is limited).

15. Relationships happen in reality, in real-time, with real people.

16. No one owes you anything in a relationship.

17. The closer you are to change, the greater will be the resistance.

18. To the degree we deny our issues, we will find a scapegoat on which to dump them.

19. Victims are focused on getting their circumstances and those around them to change, not on changing themselves.

20. Victims must be rescued; they are dependent on circumstances or others' changes to make them happy.

21. Draw a line in the sand and create a new past.

22. Give people more than they expect cheerfully.

242 Spring Park Drive, Ste A   Midland, Texas 79705   Phone: 432-682-6823   https://gr8relate.com   Email: info.gr8relate@gr8grp.com

23. Do not take things personally.

24. Be a person of your word.

25. Stop assuming what they are doing, thinking, or saying; ask questions to find out.

26. Never say I am sorry without identifying for what.

27. There are no guarantees of not being hurt in a relationship.

28. When you are in a conflict, slow your emotions down, then ask, "Am I making this about ME?"

29. Give others the freedom to be themselves.

30. Commit to little and do what you commit to do.

31. Serve others, not yourself.

32. Loving yourself and respecting yourself never needs to be developed or encouraged; it is the same as SELFISHNESS.

33. "Looking out for number 1" destroys/hurts relationships.

34. Real love involves a decision, not just emotions.

35. Love primarily based on emotions is something else – not love.

36. If you believe in falling in love, the door is open to falling out of love.

37. Do not judge, complain about, or try to change each other.

38. Pursue the best for each other and let the other person be who they are.

39. Accept the entire person – good with the bad and do not complain about the bad.

40. Practice Truth & Love in the right proportions at the right times.

41. If you are just trying to get along with them, you are probably ignoring your values.

42. If you must have it your way, you probably are ignoring freedom, grace, love, and to a large extent, the other person.

43. Emotions are incredible but remember they come primarily from your thinking.

44. Respect & trust are gifts you give to someone else.

45. Work to be trustworthy & respectable, but you cannot make others respect or trust you.

46. When trying to change others, you generally ignore changes needed in your life.

47. Apart from the grace of God, people do not change very much.

48. Look for changes in you, not changes needed in others.

49. Knowing and practicing this definition of love is the key to all good relationships "Love is pursuing their best, patiently, kindly, sacrificially and unconditionally."

50. Unconditional love is not tolerance. Love stands for truth and boundaries. Love does not rejoice in evil or what is wrong.

51. Your beliefs do not change for the better until you see current reality. Seeing current reality, things clearly, how they are, helps change our beliefs for the better.

www.ingramcontent.com/pod-product-compliance
Lightning Source LLC
Chambersburg PA
CBHW071156120626
46546CB00006B/2285